Feminist Resources for Schools and Colleges
A Guide to Curricular Materials

Revised Edition by Merle Froschl and Jane Williamson

First Edition by Carol Ahlum and Jacqueline M. Fralley

THE FEMINIST PRESS

The Clearinghouse on Women's Studies

ISBN 0-912670-14-2

This book was typeset in Press Roman and Univers by The Quick Brown Foxes, Bellmore, New York, with Americana Extra Bold heads supplied by Set To Fit, Greenwich, Connecticut. It was printed on 60# offset by Terrace Lithographers, Old Bethpage, New York.

Second edition, revised and enlarged
First edition 1973

Table of Contents

Acknowledgments

We would like to acknowledge the help of four people who contributed time and energy to this edition of *Feminist Resources.* Ilene Hertz, a year-round volunteer at The Feminist Press, helped in the early stage. Lauren Rosenbloom, a student at Kenyon College, gave up a promising career as a waitress to devote her summer to The Press and spent most of it working on *Feminist Resources.* Lucy Whittaker arrived at a crucial point near the end of the project; proofread the entire manuscript and compiled the publishers' list. Her help was indispensable. But most of all, we want to thank Jeanne Ford, Director of the Women's Center at the University of Texas/Arlington, who devoted six weeks of the summer to all phases of this project. She not only researched the material in the "Law," "Strategies for Change" and "Preschool and Elementary Education" sections, but cut, pasted and typed in true cooperative spirit. Jeanne has proven her dedication by becoming the only transcontinental volunteer The Feminist Press has ever had.

M.F./J.W.

Introduction

Feminist Resources is an annotated bibliography of nonsexist books, pamphlets, articles and other materials for teachers and students, preschool through higher education. The first edition was published in 1973 to meet the needs of and support an emerging feminist consciousness among those concerned with sex-equality in education. Since 1973, the tremendous leap both in the quantity and quality of materials has created an urgent need for an up-dated edition. The size of this new bibliography and the quality of the materials included testify to the continuing energy of feminists engaged in long-range efforts to change the education of women and men.

We began our compilation for this edition by evaluating every entry in the original *Feminist Resources*. Approximately two-thirds of these items were eliminated either because they were no longer available or because they had been replaced by newer materials. We also searched other resource guides and consulted our own rich curriculum files. Finally, we checked the catalogs of more than fifty commercial publishers and ordered all appropriate materials. Our goal throughout was to be inclusive yet selective.*

The organization of the material in the second edition has been revised in order to help readers find appropriate citations more quickly. The five major divisions are *Overview, Preschool and Elementary Education, Secondary Education, Higher Education* and *Sources of Further Information*. The *Overview* section begins with "Basic Readings" on consciousness-raising and feminist theory; five other categories within the section are "Book Studies," "For the Counselor," "Law," "Sports," "Strategies for Change." The next three sections, organized according to education level, are each divided into "Readings" and "Curriculum." Educational levels, of course, are not finite and materials listed in the section for one level may well be used in the classroom of another.

Comparing the original edition of *Feminist Resources* and this revised version reveals significant similarities and differences. This edition reaffirms the validity of the basic concept of the original editors. As Carol Ahlum and Jacqueline Fralley stated in their introduction:

This resource list is a selective guide for teachers, students, librarians and parents interested in challenging sexism in education and in creating

---

*Some of the citations in this edition are not annotated because we were unable to examine the materials first-hand. When we could not examine a piece, we would include it only if it came from a source we respected. Each annotation includes complete information with two exceptions: price and publishers' addresses. Because prices change frequently, we did not include them; publishers' addresses are listed in a separate section at the end of the publication.

nonsexist and feminist curriculum. . . . First, the entries should help teachers and others to understand the ways in which sexism is institutionalized in elementary and secondary school. Second, the list should help teachers to locate materials with which to create nonsexist and feminist curriculum.

When Ahlum and Fralley put together the first *Feminist Resources,* they noted that the majority of curriculum came from small and alternative sources. This is still true in 1976. While these "fugitive" materials are excellent, one would expect that in the past three years commercial, trade and educational publishers would have responded with excellent new materials to meet what are obviously growing demands. However, our search demonstrated that these publishers have not begun to meet these demands. In the catalogs of the more than fifty major educational publishers we examined for this edition, only one-third advertised any relevant material— and much of that did not meet our standards for inclusion. In general, commercial publishers have made superficial, not fundamental changes. For example, publishers will not rewrite an anthropology text titled, say, *Man and His World* to eliminate its pervading male bias and to add new research on women in prehistory. Instead, they might tack a filmstrip called "Women Today" on to a current affairs series. This kind of patching, plainly a simplistic reaction to pressure, currently fills publishers' catalogs with token pieces on women, blacks and other minorities. While it is important to continue to pressure for change in textbooks, it will probably also be necessary to let publishers know that a few miscellaneous filmstrips will not be adequate; that it will in fact be necessary to rewrite (not to mention retitle) *Man and His World.*

Although commercial publishers have not responded to meet the needs of teachers and students, it is still true that there are two to three times as many materials in 1976 as there were in 1973. The reasons for this growth are worth examining here, since they illuminate recent trends and help us to draw some useful general conclusions.

Perhaps the most effective force for change is the passage and implementation of Title IX, which assures that "no person . . . shall, on the basis of sex, be excluded from participation in, be denied the benefits of, or be subjected to discrimination under any education program or activity receiving federal financial assistance." The section of *Feminist Resources* which most directly reflects the response to Title IX is "Strategies for Change." The material cited there provides step-by-step guidance to help parents, teachers and school administrators make the new law a reality in their schools. Title IX also speaks to the question of equal opportunities in athletic programs and vocational channeling. We see these concerns mirrored in this edition of *Feminist Resources* in the entirely new category on "Sports" and the greatly expanded section, "For the Counselor."

Another reason for the growth in the number, scope and sophistication of materials is the growth of women's studies—research, programs, courses, teachers. Three years ago, the field of women's studies was still young and the notion of institutionalized sexism in education was relatively new. Teachers who needed help, in the form of consciousness-raising for themselves and nonsexist materials for their classroom, had a difficult and potentially fruitless search ahead. Now, research in such diverse areas as sex-role socialization, biology, history and literature has produced so significant a new body of knowledge, that the standard curriculum has to be turned inside out to incorporate it. Thus, a women's studies program on a college campus in 1976 may resemble a mini-college, with courses in most disciplines and in many interdisciplinary areas as well. There are more than 150 such programs now, compared to 75 three years ago. Women's studies has also grown off the college campus—both in the high school and the elementary classroom. More teachers are interested in nonsexist education, and as a result, are revamping their curriculum. In the past three years, we have corresponded with more than 4,000 elementary and secondary school teachers looking for new ideas and resources.

The original *Feminist Resources* attempted to draw together in one place as many of the resources as possible. Essentially, that bibliography reflected the early stages of the women's studies movement. Since then, feminist thinking and nonsexist education have advanced on all levels. It is our hope— and our intention—that this edition of *Feminist Resources* not only reflect that growth, but further it.

Overview

BASIC READINGS This section attempts to give background and consciousness-raising readings in three areas: sexism in education, sex-role socialization and its ramifications, and the general questions of the women's movement. The first section includes a wide variety of materials, many on specific topics, plus the four or five major anthologies which provide a framework for understanding the institutionalization of sexism in the schools. The section on sex-role socialization is much less comprehensive and includes only a selection of the most basic works. There is an enormous amount of periodical literature on sex roles which it did not seem useful to list fully here since access is easily available through standard indexes. The last section gives the basic books on the current women's movement, with an eye to covering all of the major issues.

SEXISM IN EDUCATION

Anderson, S. B. *Sex Differences and Discrimination in Education.* Worthington, Ohio: Charles A. Jones, 1972.

Bereaud, Susan, and Stacey, Judith, eds. *And Jill Came Tumbling After.* New York: Dell, 1974. An anthology of contemporary essays on sexism in American education from preschool through the university. Includes a valuable resource and bibliography section.

Colloquy/The Awareness Game (November 1973). A collection of popular essays and materials giving an overview of sexism in schools.

Ernest, John. *Mathematics and Sex.* 1975. Available from John Ernest. This is an excellent pamphlet on sex discrimination in mathematics teaching. A survey of women in the field of math indicates that girls are limited and stereotyped from kindergarten through graduate school.

Frazier, Nancy, and Sadker, Myra, eds. *Sexism in School and Society.* New York: Harper and Row, 1973. Written especially for teachers, this book, the only one of its kind, contains thorough but readable reviews of scientific literature on both sex roles and socialization

as well as analyses of the various aspects of sexism in schools.

Friedan, Betty, and Grant, Anne. "Sex Bias: The Built-In Mentality that Maims the Public Schools." *The American School Board Journal* 156 (October 1971):16-20.

Gersoni-Stavn, Diane, ed. *Sexism and Youth.* New York: R. R. Bowker, 1974. This 468-page anthology is in four parts: the first deals with the general question of sex-role socialization; part two covers the general atmosphere of schools; part three includes 20 studies of sexism in texts and children's books; the last section deals with toys and children's games. An excellent basic resource.

Howe, Florence. "Sexism, Racism and the Education of Women." *Today's Education* 62 (May 1973):47-48. This essay analyzes the connections between racism and sexism in schools and society.

Kampelman, Maggie. *K-12 Education Kit.* Washington: Women's Equity Action League, 1973. The purpose of the kit is to provide an overview of the central issues in sex discrimination in schools—curriculum, counseling, sports, administration. Suggests ways of effecting change.

McClure, Gail et al. "Sex Discrimination in Schools." *Today's Education* 60 (November 1971):33-35.

McCune, Shirley, ed. *Nonsexist Education for Survival*. Washington: National Education Association, 1973. This collection of working papers and reprints from the first NEA Conference on Sexism in Schools includes analyses of sexism and sex-role socialization as they are institutionalized in the school system.

Mullis, Ina V. S. *Educational Achievement and Sex Discrimination*. Denver: National Assessment of Educational Progress, 1975. This paper summarizes and analyzes the data from NAEP studies of male/female performance in a variety of subject areas. It should be accompanied by *Male/Female Achievement in Eight Learning Areas*, a compilation of selected assessment results, also available from NAEP.

National Education Association. *Sex Role Stereotyping in the Schools*. Washington: NEA. A collection of essays, a number reprinted from *Today's Education*.

New York City NOW. *Report on Sex Bias in the Public Schools*. New York: NOW, 1972. Study of Sexism in employment practices, curriculum, counseling and attitudes. Includes recommendations for change.

Phi Delta Kappan (November 1973). This special issue contains papers from the Teacher Leadership Program Conference (April 1973), focusing on the feminist movement and sexism in the schools.

Saario, Terry N.; Jacklin, Carol Nagy; and Tittle, Carol Kehr. "Sex Role Stereotyping in the Public Schools." *Harvard Educational Review* 43 (August 1973): 386-416. In this excellent article the authors investigate sex-role stereotyping in three areas: school basal readers, educational achievement tests and differential curricular requirements for males and females.

School Library Journal (January 1973). This special issue deals with subjects related to sexism in schools, such as sexism in children's books and encyclopedias and the status of librarians and high school women students.

Social Studies Journal/Sexism in Education (Winter 1973). This special issue contains articles for educators at all grade levels.

Stern, Marjorie. *Women in Education: Changing Sexist Practices in the Classroom*. Washington: American Federation of Teachers, 1972. This 75-page booklet of educational journal reprints includes three sections: "Why sexist practices should be changed," "Methods you can use in your classroom" and "Some suggested materials."

Taylor, Suzanne, ed. *The 51% Minority*. Washington: National Education Association, 1972. Papers presented at the Connecticut Education Association's first conference on women and sexism, covering the elementary school, high school women's studies, women and rock music and a consciousness-raising exercise.

Tiedt, Iris M. *Teaching for Liberation*. San Jose: Contemporary Press, 1975. Briefly discusses a variety of issues including a definition of sexism, women and work, sexism in language, sexism in children's books. It also includes ideas and methods for the classroom and suggested materials.

SEX-ROLE SOCIALIZATION

Astin, Helen; Parelman, A.; and Fisher, A. *Annotated Bibliography of Sex Roles*. Washington: National Institute of Mental Health, U. S. Public Health Service, 1974. Available from Government Printing Office.

Bradley, Mike et al. *Unbecoming Men*. New York: Times Change Press, 1971.

This 64-page pamphlet by a group of men about their childhood and adolescent socialization into sex roles is a must for parents and teachers. Be prepared for strong language.

Broverman, Inge K. et al. "Sex Role Stereotyping and Clinical Judgments of Mental Health." *Journal of Consulting and Clinical Psychiatry* 34 (February 1970):1-7. This article reports on a study of the assumptions of clinical psychiatrists and psychologists about the healthy male, the healthy female and the healthy adult.

Farrell, Warren. *The Liberated Man: Beyond Masculinity.* New York: Random House, 1974.

Fasteau, Marc Feigen. *The Male Machine.* New York: McGraw-Hill, 1974.

Horner, Matina. "Women's Will to Fail." *Psychology Today* 3 (November 1969): 37. An account of Horner's study of "women actively seeking out failure because they anticipate or expect positive consequences from failing."

Howe, Florence. "Sexual Stereotypes Start Early." *Saturday Review* 54 (October 16, 1971):76. Excellent basic analysis of sex-role socialization in society and especially its institutionalization in the schools.

Lipman-Blumen, Jean. "Changing Sex Roles in American Culture: Future Directions for Research." *Archives of Sexual Behavior* 4 (1975):433-446.

——. "How Ideology Shapes Women's Lives." *Scientific American* 226 (January 1972):34-42. Reply and rejoinder, 226 (March 1972):8. This data shows that a woman's life goals are guided by the type of sex-role ideology acquired in childhood.

——, and Tickamyer, Ann R. "Sex Roles in Transition: A Ten-Year Perspective." *Annual Review of Sociology* 1 (1975): 297-337.

Maccoby, Eleanor E. *The Development of Sex Differences.* Stanford: Stanford University Press, 1966. A classic from one of the leading sex-role researchers.

——, and Jacklin, Carol N. *The Psychology of Sex Differences.* Stanford: Stanford University Press, 1974. This book is a compilation and summary of the major research and interpretive writings in the psychological aspects of sex differences.

Maferr Foundation. *Bibliography: Male-Female Role Research.* New York: Maferr Foundation, 1974. The Maferr Foundation has sponsored research on male/female roles since 1966 and this is a bibliography of the resulting publications.

Moberg, Verne. *Consciousness Razors.* Old Westbury: The Feminist Press. A short pamphlet of funny, creative ideas for changing consciousness about sex roles; possible text in classrooms.

School Review (February 1972). This special issue features articles on new psychological and sociological research on sex differences.

Sex Roles: A Journal of Research. Editorial information: Phyllis A. Katz, Graduate School and Center of the City University, 33 W. 42 St., New York, NY 10036. Subscription information: Plenum Publishing, 227 W. 17 St., New York, NY 10011.

Spiegel, Jeanne. *Sex Role Concepts: How Women and Men See Themselves and Each Other.* Washington: Business and Professional Women's Foundation, 1969. The bibliography covers books, pamphlets, reports, theses, articles and microfilm. The material is limited to that published in the last 15 years and covers a wide spectrum—from the popular to the scholarly.

THE WOMEN'S MOVEMENT

Adams, Elsie, and Briscoe, Mary L., eds. *Up against the Wall, Mother: A Women's*

Liberation Reader. Los Angeles: Glencoe, 1971. One of the best introductory anthologies about the issues of the women's movement; includes short stories, poetry and nonfiction of both traditional and feminist views of women.

Babcox, Deborah, and Belkin, Madeline, eds. *Liberation Now!* New York: Dell, 1971. A collection of essays and articles by known and unknown writers. Women write and deal with issues, feelings and personal testimonies.

de Beauvoir, Simone. *The Second Sex.* New York: Bantam, 1970. Called the first of the recent feminist manifestoes, this book, though lengthy, is a classic and well worth reading.

Bird, Caroline. *Born Female.* New York: Pocket Books, 1968. Readable and extensive documentation of economic and political discrimination of women; good chapter on sexism and racism.

Boston Women's Health Collective. *Our Bodies, Ourselves.* New York: Simon and Schuster, 1975. This classic on women and their health and bodies has been revised and expanded. It is the best book on the subject.

Brownmiller, Susan. *Against Our Will: Men, Women and Rape.* New York: Simon and Schuster, 1975. An instant classic, this history of rape in all its aspects is a must.

Chesler, Phyllis. *Women and Madness.* New York: Avon, 1972. This book documents and explains the ramifications of sexist psychology.

Firestone, Shulamith. *The Dialectic of Sex: The Case for Feminist Revolution.* New York: Bantam, 1970. Historical, political and cultural analysis by a feminist activist of the nature and source of women's oppression.

Frankfort, Ellen. *Vaginal Politics.* New York: Quadrangle, 1972. The case for and information about women gaining control over their own bodies.

Friedan, Betty. *The Feminine Mystique.* New York: Dell, 1963. A classic; includes analysis of the exploitation of women as a so-called marginal labor force; explanation of women's manipulation by industry and advertising in the years following World War II; a clear feminist analysis of Freud's theories on women.

Gornick, Vivian, and Moran, Barbara, eds. *Women in Sexist Society: Studies in Power and Powerlessness.* New York: Basic Books, 1971. Anthology of social and psychological analyses of women's role and status.

Herschberger, Ruth. *Adam's Rib: A Defense of Modern Women.* New York: Harper and Row, 1970. This not-so-recent book (originally published in 1948) is a good introduction to feminist issues.

Hole, Judith, and Levine, Ellen. *Rebirth of Feminism.* New York: Quadrangle, 1973. Comprehensive history and analysis of the current feminist movement.

Komisar, Lucy. *The New Feminism.* New York: Paperback Library, 1972. Written especially for the high school student, this book is an introduction to the issues of the feminist movement.

Martin, Del, and Lyon, Phyllis. *Lesbian Woman.* New York: Bantam, 1972. An account of the experience of lesbians.

Miller, Casey, and Swift, Kate. *Words and Women.* New York: Anchor, 1976. A very readable book on the sexism that pervades our language.

Millett, Kate. *Sexual Politics.* New York: Avon, 1970. Analysis of the images of women in the writing of a number of male authors.

Mitchell, Juliet. *Woman's Estate.* New York: Vintage, 1973. A socialist analysis of the roots of women's oppression and the women's movement.

Morgan, Robin, ed. *Sisterhood Is Powerful.* New York: Vintage, 1970. One of the best collections of essays from the current feminist movement; includes articles by and about a variety of women: secretaries, houseworkers, prostitutes, high school women. Includes an extensive bibliography.

Nilsen, Alleen Pace et al. *Sexism and Language.* Urbana: National Council of Teachers of English, 1976.

Roszak, Betty, and Roszak, Theodore, eds. *Masculine/Feminine: Readings in Sexual Mythology and the Liberation of Women.*

New York: Harper and Row, 1970. Anthology of basic writings about women and the current women's movement.

Seaman, Barbara. *Free and Female.* New York: Fawcett, 1972. A readable book about women's sexuality.

Woolf, Virginia. *A Room of One's Own.* New York: Harcourt, 1957. An interpretation of the reasons many women have not written literature. Woolf asks, whatever happened to Shakespeare's sister? A classic.

BOOK STUDIES The first two sections in this category document the early research on sexism in books and bring it up to date with the most recent studies and reports on textbooks and trade books. Publishers have responded to this pressure and have produced guidelines for analysis of sex and race bias. These will be found in the last section, along with the newest development: evaluative instruments to help teachers and students analyze their own books.

TEXTBOOKS

Amyx, Carol. "Sex Discrimination: The Textbook Case." *California Law Review* 62 (July/September 1974):1312-1343. A well-researched article that documents the extent of sex-role stereotyping in textbooks and reports on the efforts being made to counteract the effects of these books. The author concludes that "given constitutional requirements of equality for all children . . . the obligation of those choosing textbooks for use in public schools is to choose nondiscriminatory textbooks even though there might be some sex-biased books which are considered more 'learnable.' "

Arlow, Phyllis, and Froschl, Merle. "Women in the High School Curriculum: A Review of U. S. History and English Literature Texts," in *High School Feminist Studies,* ed. Florence Howe. Old Westbury: The Feminist Press, 1976.

Written in 1973, this paper points out the need for supplementary classroom materials about women. It documents women's absence from standard history texts and the demeaning, negative roles allotted to women in literary selections used in most high school classrooms.

Baltimore Feminist Project. *Sexism and Racism in Popular Basal Readers.* New York: Racism and Sexism Resource Center for Educators, 1976. Based upon a 1973 report on the stories in five series of readers, this analysis goes far beyond a mere counting of numbers and discusses the connections between racism and sexism and their effect on all students. A 1975 postscript compares the 1973-74 Scott, Foresman *Open Highways* series with the 1965-68 version.

Beaven, Mary H. "Responses of Adolescents to Feminine Characters in Literature." *Research in the Teaching of*

English 6 (Spring 1972): 48-68. An arresting study which shows that "women in the literature read and discussed in high school English classes play minor unpleasant roles . . . The result of the survey indicates that boys and girls can relate to few of these feminine characters." This is the only survey of its kind to study the effects of female literary characters on high school students.

Burton, Gabrielle. "Sex-Role Stereotyping in Elementary School Primers." Pittsburgh: KNOW, 1974. A position paper prepared for the Montgomery County NOW, based on a review of studies conducted independently in different sections of the country. This is a good overall view of the findings of sexism in elementary textbooks. We recommend this with one reservation: the author's use of the word Negro, instead of black, throughout.

Committee to Study Sex Discrimination, Kalamazoo Public Schools. *Report of the Task Force on Elementary Textbooks.* Kalamazoo: Kalamazoo Public Schools, 1973. This study of texts, supplements and sets of study prints is one of the pioneering efforts in text analysis. It includes evaluation sheets and guidelines as well as detailed findings of the materials approved for use in the 1971-72 school year.

——. *Report of the Task Force on Selected Secondary Studies.* Kalamazoo: Kalamazoo Public Schools, 1973. An evaluation of 34 texts, paperbacks and pamphlets used in grades seven through twelve, including courses in U. S. history, English, anthropology, homemaking, mass media. Evaluation and interview sheets are included.

Education Task Force, National Organization for Women, Lexington Chapter. *Putting Women in Their Place: Report on American History High School Textbooks.* Lexington, Mass.: NOW, 1976. Based on a study of 30 high school texts, this report includes detailed reviews of nine books, a special study of the colonial period, questions and assignments, a list of notable American women and a bibliography.

Feminists on Children's Media. *Sexism in Children's Books: A Bibliography.* Pittsburgh: KNOW, 1974. A selective list of articles on sexism in children's books, including only those pieces with original ideas or research. Includes studies of picture books, trade books and fairy tales, as well as texts.

Frasher, Ramona, and Walker, Annabelle. "Sex Roles in Early Reading Textbooks." *The Reading Teacher* 25 (May 1972): 741-749. An analysis of first- and second-grade readers and readiness books from four major basal reading series.

Frisof, Jamie Kelem. "Textbooks and Channeling." *Women: A Journal of Liberation* 1 (Fall 1969):26-28. An analysis of five modern social studies textbooks for grades one to three from: Macmillan, Prentice-Hall, D. C. Heath, Science Research Associates, Allyn and Bacon.

Graebner, Dianne Bennett. "A Decade of Sexism in Readers." *The Reading Teacher* 6 (October 1972):52-58. Study of sexism in Scott, Foresman and Ginn elementary reader series.

Kraft, Linda. "Lost Herstory: The Treatment of Women in Children's Encyclopedias." *School Library Journal* 19 (January 1973):26-35.

Lysne, Ruth, and Warner, Margo. "A Women's Place: What's Cooking in Junior High School English Anthologies." *Minnesota English Journal* 8 (Fall 1972): 27-41. A well-documented study, with many examples, that raises questions concerning the portrayal of women in the books used either as basic or supplemental texts. Twenty anthologies from major publishing houses were surveyed and charted for this article.

Macleod, Jennifer S., and Silverman, Sandra T. *You Won't Do: What Textbooks on U. S. Government Teach High School Girls.* Pittsburgh: KNOW, 1973. A documentation of women's absence in civics textbooks. This 109-page paperback recommends actions for changing curriculum and includes an annotated bibliography of studies about women in textbooks.

Michigan Women's Commission. *Sex Discrimination in an Elementary Reading Program.* Lansing: Michigan Women's Commission, 1974. A comprehensive report based on the work of the Committee to Study Sex Discrimination in the Kalamazoo Public Schools. The textbooks under scrutiny were the 12 texts in the elementary reading program published by Houghton-Mifflin. This booklet includes the complaint filed and correspondence with Caspar Weinberger, at HEW, as well as tables and a bibliography.

Mullen, Jean S. "Freshman Textbooks." *College English* 34 (October 1972): 79-93. A survey of 112 textbooks, issued by 18 publishers, which documents the underrepresentation of women writers used in college freshman English classes.

National Education Association. *Cassette Tape—Minorities and Women in Instructional Materials.* Washington: NEA.

O'Donnell, Richard W. "Sex Bias in Primary Social Studies Textbooks." *Educational Leadership* 31 (November 1973): 137-141. A study of the six basic texts for first and second grades in one school district's 1971-72 approved list.

Racism and Sexism Resource Center for Educators. *Feminist Packet.* New York: Racism and Sexism Resource Center for Educators. Reprints from various issues of the *Bulletin,* including: "Feminists View 100 Books," "Women in Textbooks," "Sexism in Textbooks" and "Pippi Longstocking: Feminist or Anti-Feminist?"

Schmidt, Dolores. "Sexism in Education," in *Female Studies V,* ed. Rae Lee Siporin. Pittsburgh: KNOW, 1972. Review of studies on sexism in a variety of books that affect the self-image of girls throughout their education. Included are children's books, the elementary history text, the high school and college literature anthology.

Stefflre, Buford. "Run, Mamma, Run: Women Workers in Elementary Readers." *Vocational Guidance Quarterly* 18 (December 1969):99-102. Analysis of the extent to which adult females are shown as workers in six major reading series and the extent to which the reality of the readers replicates the reality of women in the work force.

Trecker, Janice Law. "Women in U. S. History High School Textbooks." *Social Education* 35 (March 1971):247. The first and most extensive documentation of the women who do not appear in history books—and why.

U'Ren, Marjorie. "Image of Women in Textbooks," in *Woman in Sexist Society,* ed. Vivian Gornick and Barbara K. Moran. New York: Basic Books, 1971. Report of a study of 30 recently published school texts adopted or recommended for use in California schools.

Weitzman, Lenore J., and Rizzo, Diane. *Biased Textbooks.* Washington: Resource Center on Sex Roles in Education, 1975. Documents the omission and stereotyping of females in textbooks in five subject areas and suggests actions for teachers and parents.

——. *Images of Males and Females in Elementary School Textbooks.* Available from The Feminist Press and The

Resource Center on Sex Roles in Education. This lively slide show (with music) is based on two years of comprehensive research focusing on the latent content of texts. The show analyzes the most widely used textbooks in the United States in science, mathematics, reading, spelling and social studies, according to age, race and sex.

Wiik, Susan L. "The Sexual Bias of Textbook Literature." *English Journal* 62 (February 1973):224-229. Examination of 15 literature anthologies frequently used in junior high school classrooms.

Women on Words and Images. *Dick and Jane as Victims: Sex Stereotypes in Children's School Readers.* Princeton: Women on Words and Images, 1972. Now a classic, this study gives a lengthy, detailed report on 134 elementary school readers used in school systems throughout the country. Also available as a 30-minute slide/tape show with cassette. Revised and expanded in 1976.

——. *Sexism in Foreign Language Textbooks.* Princeton: Women on Words and Images, 1975. This slide show explores the sexist content of 25 French, Spanish and German textbooks.

TRADE BOOKS

Bernstein, Joanne. "Changing Roles of Females in Books for Young Children." *The Reading Teacher* 27 (March 1974): 545-549.

Czaplinski, Suzanne M. *Sexism in Award-Winning Picture Books.* Pittsburgh: KNOW, 1973. The author reviews previous articles on sexism in picture books, looks at the psychological implications of early sex stereotypes, analyzes the award-winning Caldecott and Carroll books. Included is a time study that analyzes the 60-book sampling in regard to the changes in sex bias from the 1940's to the present.

Feminists on Children's Media. "A Feminist Look at Children's Books." *School Library Journal* 18 (January 1971): 19-24. One of the first analyses of sexism in children's books, this article examines the highly recommended Newbery award winners.

Fisher, Elizabeth. "The Second Sex, Junior Division." *The New York Times Book Review* (May 24, 1970):6. A brief, incisive analysis of sexism in picture books.

Forth Worth Education Task Force, NOW. *This Book Is Rated S* (*Sexist).* Available from Fort Worth Education Task Force, NOW. An 18-minute slide show about sexism in children's literature from preschool books through teen-age novels.

Heyn, Leah. "Children's Books." *Women: A Journal of Liberation* 1 (Fall 1969): 22-25. Discussion of sex stereotyping in a variety of children's books.

Howe, Florence. "Liberated Chinese Primers (Let's Write Some Too)." *Women: A Journal of Liberation* 2 (Fall 1970):33-34. Analysis of sex roles in several Chinese picture books for children.

Key, Mary Ritchie. "The Role of Male and Female in Children's Books: Dispelling All Doubt." *Wilson Library Bulletin* 46 (October 1971):167-176. Overview of a number of studies on sexism in children's books.

Lewis, Susan. "Exploding the Fairy Princess Myth." *Scholastic Teacher/Elementary Edition* (November 1971):11. Discussion of sexism in children's books; bibliography included.

Lieberman, Marcia. "Someday My Prince Will Come: Female Acculturation through Fairy Tales." *College English* 34 (December 1972):383-398. Incisive analysis of sexism in time-honored fairy tales.

Matthews, Dorothy. "An Adolescent's Glimpse of the Faces of Eve." *Illinois*

English Bulletin 60 (May 1973):1. A
study of the image of women in selected
popular junior novels. The author's con-
clusion is that "in most junior novels
girls are brainwashed to accept their in-
ferior station in society . . . English
teachers should become more sensitive
to sexist propaganda."

Nilsen, Alleen Pace. "Women in Children's
Literature." *College English* 32 (May
1971):918-926. Survey of 1951-1970
winners and runners-up in the Caldecott
competition.

Racism and Sexism Resource Center for
Educators. *Human Values in Children's
Books.* New York: Racism and Sexism
Resource Center for Educators, 1976.
The first volume of an annual series that
will examine each year's juvenile books
on minority, feminist and social-issue
themes. This volume analyzes more than
200 books to identify what values
they transmit to young people.

Stavn, Diane Gersoni. "The Skirts in
Fiction about Boys: A Maxi Mess."
School Library Journal 18 (January
1971):62-72. Description of the portrayal of girls and women in books
popular among boys.

———. "On Feminist Criticism: An Overview." *School Library Journal* 20
(January 1974):22. The importance of
feminist criticism of children's books.

Stewig, John, and Higgs, Margaret. "Girls
Grow Up to Be Mommies: A Study of
Sexism in Children's Literature." *School
Library Journal* 19 (January 1973):
44-49. One hundred and fifty-four picture books are surveyed here, chosen as
"representative of those typically available to children in school and public
libraries."

Tibbetts, Sylvia-Lee. "Children's Literature: A Feminist's Viewpoint." *California Journal of Educational Research*
26 (January 1975):1-5.

Training Institute for Sex Desegregation of
the Public Schools. *Free to Read.* New
Brunswick: Training Institute for Sex
Desegregation of the Public Schools,
1976. Slide show highlighting nonsexist,
nonracist picture books for ages three to
nine.

Vukelich, Carol; McCarty, Charlotte; and
Nanis, Claire. "Sex Bias in Children's
Books." *Childhood Education* 52 (February 1976):220-222. Although professional literature reflects a concern, dating
back to 1971, about sex stereotyping in
books written for children, this research
suggests that, to date, teachers appear
not to be evaluating picture books for
sex roles.

Weitzman, Lenore J. et al. *Sex-Role
Socialization in Picture Books for Pre-
School Children.* Pittsburgh: KNOW,
1971. Examination of sex-role socialization of young children in the Caldecott
and Newbery award winners, Little
Golden Books and etiquette books.

GUIDELINES AND ANALYSES

"Any Change in Sexist Texts?" *Women's
Studies Newsletter* 2 (Summer 1974):1.
A report on interviews conducted in the
spring of 1974 with 15 major educational
publishers. The publishers discuss their
plans and attitudes toward the sexist bias
of their texts.

Committee on the Role and Image of
Women in the Council and the Profession, The National Council of Teachers
of English. *Guidelines for Publications.*
Urbana: NCTE, 1973. A how-to flyer
of guidelines for representing half the
human race in the written word. A good
resource for English teachers. Also
available is a new seven-page
booklet, *Guidelines for Nonsexist Use
of Language in NCTE Publications,* reprinted from the March 1976 *Language
Arts, English Journal* and *College English.*

Lewis, Jennifer. "What the Publishers Are

Doing about Sexism in Textbooks."
Teacher 90 (October 1972):52-53. An
article which reports on interviews with
Harper and Row, Ginn, Heath, Houghton-
Mifflin, Macmillan and Lippincott.

Massachusetts Department of Education.
*A Guide for the Evaluation of Instruc-
tional Materials Under Chapter 622.*
Boston: Massachusetts Department of
Education, 1975. This booklet is designed to aid school personnel to identify racial and sexual stereotyping in
materials. It contains sheets and checklists for evaluating fiction, readers,
mathematics texts, science books,
social studies texts. A selected bibliography is included.

National Education Association. *How
Fair Are Your Children's Textbooks?*
Washington: NEA, n.d. Available from
American Education Week. A pamphlet
listing questions to ask to insure that
basic educational materials accurately
portray our country's cultural diversity
and properly reflect the various contributions of minority groups and
women.

New York State Education Department.
Reviewing Curriculum for Sexism.
Albany: New York State Education Department, 1975. Initiated by the Task
Force on Equal Opportunity for Women,
these 88-page guidelines outline the procedures used by the New York State
Education Department in examining its
own publications for sexism. Included
are suggestions for eliminating sex bias
in instructional materials.

Racism and Sexism Resource Center for
Educators. *Stereotypes, Distortions and
Omissions in U. S. History Textbooks:
A Content Analysis Instrument for
Detecting Racism and Sexism.* New
York: Racism and Sexism Resource Cen-
ter for Educators, 1976. Contains de-
tailed charts against which you can check

a textbook's treatment of African Americans, Asian Americans, Native Americans,
Mexican Americans, Puerto Ricans—and
women of all groups. The charts list the
most common errors which appear in
elementary and secondary American
history books, and provide information
to counteract the bias against racism
and sexism.

——. *Ten Quick Ways to Analyze Children's Books for Racism and Sexism.*
Racism and Sexism Resource Center for
Educators, 1974. Flyer for teachers,
librarians, parents and students that
offers easy-to-use methods for evaluating stereotypes, distortions and omissions frequently found in school and
library books.

Task Force for the Evaluation of Instructional Materials. *A Guide to Textbook
Evaluation.* Stanford: Task Force for the
Evaluation of Instructional Materials,
1974. An aid to help evaluate materials
for sex, race and ethnic bias. Includes a
sample analysis of books from more than
a dozen publishers, and suggests follow-
up activities if there is no alternative to
using biased materials.

Publishers Guidelines. Several publishing
companies have developed guidelines to
help eliminate sex- and race-stereotyping
in their books. The following companies
have such free materials: Holt, Rinehart
and Winston, *Guidelines for the Development of Elementary and Secondary Instructional Materials;* Houghton-Mifflin,
Avoiding Stereotypes; Macmillan, *Guidelines for Creating Positive Sexual and
Racial Images in Educational Materials;*
McGraw-Hill, *Guidelines for Equal Treatment of the Sexes;* Science Research Associates, *Suggestions for Developing
Materials that are Free of Racial, Sexual,
Cultural and Social Bias;* Scott, Foresman,
*Guidelines for Improving the Image of
Women in Textbooks.*

FOR THE COUNSELOR The counseling section is organized into three parts: general readings, career information and statistics. These correspond with the major areas of concern to counselors: self-awareness, career awareness and labor market trends. Although this section is designated "For the Counselor," we realize that everyone is a counselor at some point— teachers, administrators, librarians. Therefore, we recommend that everyone look through this section for appropriate material. Likewise, we recommend that counselors read the curriculum sections since they will find relevant materials there as well.

GENERAL READINGS

Abt Publications. *Sex Fairness in Career Guidance: A Learning Kit.* Cambridge: Abt Publications, 1975. Developed for use by counselors, teachers, administrators and librarians under contract from the National Institute for Education, this extensive curriculum contains: Orientation to Sex-Fairness, Recommendations for a Comprehensive Sex-Fair Career Guidance Program, Guidelines and Recommendations for Sex-Fair Use of Career Interest Inventories, A Resource Guide. The annotated resource guide provides a complete reference to readings and audiovisual materials; a cassette with supplementary exercises is also included.

"AMEG Commission Report on Sex Bias in Interest Measurement." *Measurement and Evaluation in Guidance* 6 (October 1973):171-177. This report addresses important considerations about sex bias relevant to all interest inventories and examines possible sex bias in the Strong Vocational Interest Blanks and its revision, Strong-Campbell Interest Inventory.

American Personnel and Guidance Association. This organization has developed a variety of materials useful for counseling women:

Assertive Training Procedures for Women. 1973. This film series describes methods which enable girls and women to stand up for their basic human rights. Two companion paperbacks contain enough relevant material to be used on their own: "An Introduction to Assertive Training Procedures for Women," "Leader's Guide to Assertive Training for Women."

Back to School, Back to Work. 1973. A film that focuses on counseling women in transition from, for example, housewife to student or mother to career woman. Theory, discussion questions and models are presented in the 24-page "Leader's Guide."

Counseling Girls and Women over the Lifespan. 1972. This 96-page book is designed to promote the awareness, understanding and knowledge needed to counsel girls and women.

Facilitating Career Development for Girls and Women. 1973. A monograph of the National Vocational Guidance Association including: "Historical Perspectives," "Expanding Career Options for Females" and "Young Children's Perceptions of Occupational Roles." All selections have extensive bibliographies.

Women and Counselors (October 1972). This special issue of *Personnel and Guidance Journal* provides a complete framework for counseling women. It states the problems, proposes solutions and suggests steps for implementation. Includes articles on the elementary school, working women and sexism and racism.

Bem, Sandra, and Bem, Daryl. *Homogenizing the American Woman: The Power of Nonconscious Idealogy.* Pittsburgh: KNOW, 1972. Recently revised, expanded and retitled, this article is a clear explanation of the effect of sex-role conditioning on women's aspirations. Includes an analysis of the child's socialization at home and in school.

Birk, J., and Tanney, M. *Career Exploration for High School Women: A Model.* ERIC, 1972. This paper, presented at the National Education Association Conference at Airlie, Virginia, is a curriculum model for junior and senior high school designed to heighten awareness of the influence of sexism on women's roles.

Briggs, Norma. *Women in Apprenticeship— Why Not?* Washington: Manpower Administration, U. S. Department of Labor, 1974. Available from Government Printing Office. A report on a project in Wisconsin to "isolate, analyze and minimize barriers to women in the skilled trades."

Business and Professional Women's Foundation. *Career Counseling: New Perspectives for Women and Girls.* Washington: Business and Professional Women's Foundation, 1972. A selected annotated bibliography that describes more than 100 books, reports and articles, including research material on counseling and occupational choices.

"Career Planning for High School Girls." *Occupational Outlook Quarterly* 17 (Summer 1973). An article that looks at the importance of career planning and exploring nontraditional occupations for high school women.

The Center for Vocational Education, The Ohio State University. The Center has produced a variety of publications related to women in the world of work:

Implications of Women's Work Patterns for Program Development in Vocational-Technical Education. Sylvia L. Lee et al. 1967.

High School Senior Girls and the World of Work: Occupational Knowledge, Attitudes and Plans. Sylvia L. Lee et al. 1971.

Planning Ahead for the World of Work— Curriculum Materials. Louise Vetter and Barbara J. Sethney. 1975.

Women in the Work Force: Development and Field Testing of Curriculum Materials. Louise Vetter and Barbara J. Sethney. 1972.

Career Guidance Materials: Implications for Women's Career Development. Louise Vetter, David Stockburger and Christine Brose. 1974.

Implications for Women's Work Patterns for Vocational and Technical Education: An Annotated Bibliography. Sylvia L. Lee et al. 1967.

Women in the World of Work: A Bibliography of ERIC Documents. Paul E. Schroeder. 1973.

Review and Synthesis of Research on Women in the World of Work. Mary Back Kievit. 1972.

Women in the Work Force: Follow-Up Study of Curriculum Materials. Louise Vetter, Alice J. Brown and Barbara J. Sethney. 1975.

The Counselor and the Feminine Protest. ERIC, 1971. (CG 400 034). A program originally presented at the 1971 American Personnel and Guidance Association National Convention. Included are role-playing situations and speeches that dramatize the difficulties faced by counselors as a result of their own sex-role conditioning and conflicts.

Diamond, Eleanor, ed. *Issues of Sex Bias and Sex Fairness in Career Interest Management.* Washington: National Institute of Education, 1975. A series of in-depth papers with bibliographies which represent a comprehensive analysis of sex bias in measurements and inventories. Included are the guidelines developed to combat sex bias in interest measurements.

ERIC Counseling and Personnel Services Information Center, School of Education, Room 2108, University of Michigan, Ann Arbor, MI 48104. One of the 16 ERIC Clearinghouses that contain current educational materials. Write for information on women and counseling.

Farmer, Helen, and Backer, Thomas. *New Career Options for Women: A Three-Part Counseling Series.* Los Angeles: Human Interaction Research Institute, 1976. Sponsored by the National Institute of Education, this series is comprised of three components: *A Counselor's Sourcebook, Things Are Looking Up* (an illustrated, 60-page condensed version of the Sourcebook) and a *Selected Annotated Bibliography.*

Gardner, Jo-Ann. "Sexist Counseling Must Stop." *Personnel and Guidance Journal* 49 (May 1971):705-713. An appeal for a change in counseling, the article includes a useful chart listing the similarities between two oppressed groups: women and blacks.

Green, Cynthia P. *The Choice Is Yours.* 1975. Available from Cynthia Green. This 128-page xeroxed resource kit contains supplementary printed materials and suggestions for audio-visual materials. The four units cover: the status of women, role options for women, self-awareness and career development. It can be used as a women's studies course for noncollege-bound high school students.

Guidance Associates. This organization has developed several good filmstrip series on sex-fair counseling that would be useful in interdisciplinary women's studies courses. Each contains two filmstrips, plus records or cassettes, and a discussion guide:

Jobs and Gender. Explores ways in which gender may influence vocational choices: discusses changing concepts of "masculine" and "feminine" work roles.
Women Today. 1975. Presents various women with strong, positive self-images who have made conscious life choices. Will help students look at themselves and at their sex prejudices and stereotypes.
Women at Work: Choice and Challenge. 1976. Explores the changing roles of women in the labor force and the challenges these changes have generated. Presents a detailed documentary of women's work roles from colonial times to the present; examines changing work patterns in the 70's.

Jeghelian, Alice. "Surviving Sexism: Strategies and Consequences." *Personnel and Guidance Journal* 54 (February 1976):307-311. Advice to counselors to help women who decide to confront sexism in institutions. Includes an affirmative action case study, "Sexism in Institutions of Higher Education."

Journals. A number of professional journals have published special issues on sex roles and counseling: *American Journal of Orthopsychiatry* 41 (October 1971), *Personnel and Guidance Journal* 51 (October 1972), *Contact* 3 (Fall 1972), *The Counseling Psychologist* 4 (1973), *American Journal of Sociology* 78 (1973).

Mitchell, Joyce Slayton. *Other Choices for Becoming a Woman.* Pittsburgh: KNOW, 1974. A feminist handbook for high school women to help them realize their potential and plan for the future. Especially useful are the sections on educational choices in and out of high school.

National Institute of Education, Education and Work Group. *Guidelines for Assessment of Sex Bias and Sex Fairness in Career Interest Inventories.* Washington:

U. S. Department of Health, Education and Welfare, 1974. The guidelines developed as part of the NIE Career Education Program are presented in three sections: Inventory, Technical Information, Interpretive Information.

Nickerson, Eileen T. *Counseling Women Today for Tomorrow.* Available from Eileen Nickerson. Collected papers of the conference sponsored by the Status of Women Committee, the Massachusetts Personnel and Guidance Association, 1973.

Nontraditional Careers for Women. Filmstrips and cassettes. Pathescope Educational Films.

Oliver, Laurel W. "Counseling Implications of Recent Research on Women." *Personnel and Guidance Journal* 53 (February 1975):430-437. Survey of recent research on women in four areas: counselor bias, demographic changes, sex differences, sex-role stereotypes. Includes suggestions for counselors who wish to increase their sensitivity to the issues raised.

Project on Sex Equality in Guidance Opportunities, American Personnel and Guidance Association. *A Chance to Choose.* This filmstrip on counseling is included in the multi-media kit developed by the SEGO project. Distribution information can be obtained by writing to the Office of Education, Department of Health, Education and Welfare.

Project on Status and Education of Women. *American Personnel and Guidance Association Cites Vocational Test for Sex Bias.* Washington: Project on the Status and Education of Women, 1972. A copy of the unprecedented ruling presented at the APGA annual meeting in March 1972, in which the Strong Vocational Interest Blank was cited as being discriminatory and was slated for revision.

San Fernando Valley AAUW *Great Expectations.* Available from Center for New Directions. A packet of exercises for young women about the future and work.

Schlossberg, Nancy K., and Goodman, Jane. "A Woman's Place: Children's Sex Stereotyping of Occupations." *Vocational Guidance Quarterly* 120 (June 1972):266-270. Reviews a study of children's perceptions of jobs appropriate for women and men.

Scholz, Nelle; Prince, Judith; and Miller, Gordon. *How to Decide: A Guide for Women.* New York: College Entrance Examination Board, 1976. A how-to workbook, using case studies, charts, checkpoints, inventories and simulation games to help women of any age improve their decision-making abilities in regard to home, family and work. Sex-role stereotyping is an important consideration throughout.

Scott, Jeanne, and Rabin, Maureen. *The Vocational Readiness Package.* Available from Jeanne Scott. A five-day program for junior and senior high school women utilizing simulation games and improvisational drama to stimulate more realistic thinking about careers and marriage.

Steele, M. *Women in Vocational Education: Project Baseline Supplementary Report.* 1975. Available from M. Steele. Reviews and analyzes available data on women in vocational education with recommendations for change.

Stevenson, Gloria. "Counseling Black Teenage Girls—A Human Experience." *Occupational Outlook Quarterly* 19 (Summer 1974). A summary of the research on the differing educational and job-market experiences of young black and young white women.

Tiedt, Iris M. "Realistic Counseling for High School Girls." *The High School Counselor* 19 (May 1972):54-56. An overview of the problems of counseling high school women.

Vancouver Status of Women. *Exploring Sex-Typing: A Kit for Counselors.* Available from Vancouver Status of Women. A kit with a variety of methods and materials for counselors to use with groups of young people.

When I Grow Up I'm Going to Get Married. Available from Michigan State University, Counseling Center. A game for teen-age girls, developed to create an awareness of the realities of life. Based on statistics, ten profiles give students experience in planning for ways to deal with a variety of life situations.

Wolkon, Kenneth A, *Counseling Girls and Women: A Guide for Jewish and Other Minority Women.* Washington: B'nai B'rith, 1973. This pamphlet discusses the women's movement and the issue of job discrimination. It suggests the following counseling considerations: What is women's role in our society? What should it be?

Women on Words and Images. *Help Wanted: Sexism in Career Education Materials.* Princeton: Women on Words and Images, 1975. An analysis of the sexism found in a study of 100 career education materials. A slide show of the same title which focuses on how females and males are stereotypically tracked into traditional careers is also available.

Women's Task Force, American College Personnel Association of the American Personnel and Guidance Association. Available from Nancy L. Balick. A paper prepared by this organization gives the background and functions of the Task Force.

YWCA. *A Job at the End: Guidelines for Teen Counseling, Training and Career Development.* New York: YWCA, 1975. In 1973, the Resource Center on Women of the YWCA conducted a research pro-

ject which revealed that "81% of the teen women interviewed listed job counseling as their top priority need." This book offers specifics for setting up local job placement and career development programs for teen women. Two earlier booklets published under this project are also available: *Attention Is Needed, Action Is Called For* and *Let's Try a Workshop with Teen Women.*

CAREER INFORMATION

Alpha Kappa Alpha Sorority. *Heritage Series.* Chicago: AKA Sorority. Five free booklets with photographs and short biographies recount the work of professional women in the judiciary, politics, business, medicine and dentistry.

American College Testing Program. *Women in Science and Technology: Careers for Today and Tomorrow.* Iowa City: American College Testing Program, 1976. Depicts women who have careers in the field of science and technology and discusses the myths and realities of these careers.

Campbell, Margaret. *Why Would a Girl Go into Medicine?* Old Westbury: The Feminist Press, 1973. A survey of women's experiences in 41 medical schools across the country which provides an invaluable guide to the unpleasant realities and encouraging solutions for women entering the medical professions.

Fenten, D. X. *Ms-Attorney.* Philadelphia: Westminster Press, 1974. Examines the discrimination against women in the field of law and gives a brief history of law from primitive societies to the present. A list of American law schools with admission requirements and costs is included.

——. *Ms-M.D.* Philadelphia: Westminster Press, 1973. A discussion of the prejudices that women face in medical training and practice, along with practical information concerning scholastic preparation, required training, medical schools and tuition costs.

Medsger, Betty. *Women at Work.* New York: Sheed and Ward, 1975. A beautiful photographic documentary of hundreds of women across the United States doing the work women have always done. The factory worker, household worker, teacher, office worker, coal miner, blacksmith and garage mechanic are all included. Thoughtful essays and comments accompany the photographs of women at their jobs.

Mitchell, Joyce Slayton. *I Can Be Anything: Careers and Colleges for Young Women.* New York: College Entrance Examination Board, 1975. Description of a wide range of traditional and nontraditional careers for women—from airline pilot to zoologist. For each of the 92 fields, information is given on salaries, education and future prospects.

Project Equality. *But What Can I Do?* Seattle: Highline Public School District, 1974. Thirteen filmstrip-cassette presentations give basic information concerning the duties and responsibilities of women and men in nontraditional crafts and professions.

Seed, Susanne. *Saturday's Child.* New York: Bantam, 1974. Thirty-six women photographed and interviewed about their nontraditional jobs share personal backgrounds, feelings and anecdotes.

Splaver, Sarah. *Nontraditional Careers for Women.* New York: Julian Messner, 1973. Five hundred career possibilities are discussed, including legal fields, medicine, education, clergy, math, science, engineering, business, manual trades, government.

Women's Bureau, U. S. Department of Labor. This agency has several publications available on career opportunities for women: *Selected Sources of Career Information,* 1974; *Steps to Opening the Skilled Trades to Women,* 1974; *Careers for Women in the 70's,* 1973; *Counseling Women for Careers in Business,* 1973; *Look Who's Wearing Lipstick!,* 1972; *Why Not Be—an Apprentice,* 1974; *Why Not Be—a Medical Technologist,* 1971; *Why Not Be—a Technical Writer,* 1971; *Why Not Be—an Optometrist,* 1968.

Women's Work, Washington Opportunities for Women, 1111 20 St. N.W., Washington, DC 20036. A bi-monthly publication with regular columns on employment, trends, jobs, career ideas.

Many women professionals have formed their own associations and have free or inexpensive career planning materials specifically for girls and women. Among them are:

American Home Economics Association, 2010 Massachusetts Ave. N.W., Washington, DC 20036.

American Medical Women's Association, 1740 Broadway, New York, NY 10019.

Boalt Hall Women's Association, School of Law, University of California, Berkeley, CA 94720.

Council on Dental Education, American Dental Association, 211 E. Chicago Ave., Chicago, IL 60611.

National League for Nursing, 10 Columbus Circle, New York, NY 10019.

Women in Communications, Inc., 8305-A, Shoal Creek Blvd., Austin, TX 78758.

Women Leaders Round Table of the National Association of Life Underwriters, 1922 F St. N.W., Washington, DC 20006.

STATISTICS

Bureau of the Census, U. S. Department of Commerce. *A Statistical Portrait of Women in the U. S.* 1975. Available

from Government Printing Office. A
variety of data bearing on the changing
social and economic status of women
in the United States.

———. *We the American Women*. 1973.
Available from Government Printing
Office. Statistical profile of women in
American society today.

Bureau of Labor Statistics, U. S. Department of Labor. *U. S. Working Women:
A Chartbook.* 1975. Available from
Government Printing Office. A wide
array of data (56 charts) on the characteristics of the American working
woman and her changing status over the
past quarter of a century.

The Conference Board. *Women: A Demographic, Social and Economic Presentation.* New York: The Conference Board,
1973. A handy booklet of charts concerning the status of women, including
age of marriage, marital status, women as
household heads, housework, women in
the labor force.

National Education Association. *Sex-Role
Stereotyping Fact Sheets.* Washington:
NEA.

Women's Bureau, U. S. Department of
Labor. *Handbook on Women Workers.*
1975. Available from Government Printing Office. An excellent source of
statistics. Charts and tables supplement
facts relating to the present economic,
civil and political status of women.

SPORTS   This category reflects the growing interest in sports for girls and
women and lists a wide variety of materials including books, articles,
conference reports, periodicals, organizations and curricular materials.

Committee to Study Sex Discrimination,
Kalamazoo Public Schools. The Kalamazoo schools have four documents relating to sports and physical education
available as a result of their efforts to
eliminate sex discrimination: *In Search
of the Freedom to Grow* (1973), the report of their physical education/athletics
task force which details their work and
recommendations; *Program Plan to Implement Title IX Physical Education
Program Provisions* (1975), suggests
changes to be made year by year on all
levels; *Revised Physical Education Program for Junior and Senior High Schools*
(1975), the new program designed by
the Department of Physical Education
which outlines overall and specific goals
for each grade as well as plans for meeting them; *Master Plan for Men's and Women's Athletics* (1975), a master chart
of the program and schedule. All are
good models.

Division for Girls and Women's Sports,
American Association for Health, Physical Education and Recreation, 1201
16 St. N.W., Washington, DC 20036. A
good source for all kinds of information
on girls and women in sports.

Equity in School Athletics: A Guide. New
Brunswick: Training Institute for Sex
Desegregation of the Public Schools,
Douglass College, 1976.

Gerber, Ellen et al. *The American Woman
in Sport.* Reading, Mass.: Addison-
Wesley, 1974. Comprehensive and
definitive text on American women in
sport, including some original research
and some synthesis of the research of
others. Sections on history, society's
attitudes, portrait of the woman athlete
and the biophysical perspective.

Good Sports. New Brunswick: Training Institute for Sex Desegregation of the Public Schools, 1976. Slide show.

Hoepner, Barbara, J., ed. *Women's Athletics: Coping with Controversy.* Washington: American Association for Health, Physical Education and Recreation, 1974.

Journal of Health, Physical Education and Recreation. The activities and research of the Division for Girls and Women's Sports are regularly reported in this journal of the American Association for Health, Physical Education and Recreation.

Levy, Maury Z. "The Girls of Summer." *WomenSports* 1 (August 1974):37-39. This brief article on the fight to have girls admitted into Little League teams summarizes the issues and describes the cases of several girls. Good consciousness-raising reading for parents, teachers, coaches and students.

Lichtenburg, Margaret Klee. "Books," *WomenSports* 1 (September 1974):69. A very useful review article on recent fiction and nonfiction about sportswomen for young readers.

Project on the Status and Education of Women. *What Constitutes Equality for Women in Sport?* Washington: Project on the Status and Education of Women, 1975. This excellent paper outlines the issues related to equal opportunity for women in sport, gives a good summary of the legal mandate and explores some of the alternatives that have been proposed. College level, includes an excellent bibliography.

"Revolution in Women's Sports." *WomenSports* 1 (September 1974). This 22-page report covers all aspects of sports in school as well as the professional scene, including information on Title IX, an action manual for eliminating discrimination in school sports programs, discussion of the origins of sexist attitudes and more. One of the best resources around. Available as a reprint from the Women's Sports Foundation (see below).

Skidmore, Patricia. *Women in Sports.* Washington: Women's Equity Action League, 1975. This "sports kit" includes information on Title IX, on filing discrimination complaints, on federal law and has a bibliography.

The Sportswoman, Jensen-Fane Publications, 6150 Buckingham Pkwy., Culver City, CA 90807.

Task Force on Women in Sports, NOW, 5 S. Wabash, #1615, Chicago, IL 60603. A good resource.

Women in Sports. Available from Cathy Cade. Six durable 8" x 10" reproductions of women skilled in gymnastics, softball, track, weight-lifting and judo. Suggestions for using the photos in the classroom included.

Women's Rights Project, American Civil Liberties Union. *Sex Discrimination in Athletics and Physical Education.* New York: ACLU, forthcoming. The packet is being revised and will be available January 1977.

WomenSports, 1660 S. Amphlett Blvd., San Mateo, CA 94402. Monthly magazine which is an excellent resource for all teachers and students. A must in all school libraries.

Women's Sports Foundation, 1660 S. Amphlett Blvd., #266, San Mateo, CA 94402. The Women's Sports Foundation was founded in 1974 as a public, nonprofit corporation by Billie Jean King to "encourage all women to be involved in sport activities." The Foundation's services and programs include an information and referral center, a comprehensive library, encouragement and backing of competitions and clinics for women, support for research and financial aid. A quarterly newsletter is sent to all members; write for complete information.

LAW This section is in two parts: the first is very brief and lists guides to women's legal rights generally; the second concerns itself with the legislation regarding sex discrimination in the schools.

WOMEN'S LEGAL RIGHTS

Alexander, Shana. *State-by-State Guide to Women's Legal Rights.* Los Angeles: Wollstonecraft, 1975.

Leary, Denise Brender, comp. *Federal Laws and Regulations Prohibiting Sex Discrimination.* Washington: Women's Equity Action League, 1976. This 22" by 35" wall chart lists eight federal laws and regulations with information about coverage, filing complaints and sources of further information.

Ross, Susan. *The Rights of Women: The Basic ACLU Guide to a Woman's Rights.* New York: E. P. Dutton, 1973. A readable, comprehensive guide in question and answer format to the legal rights of women.

U. S. Department of Health, Education and Welfare, Office for Civil Rights. *Sex Discrimination.* Washington: U. S. Department of HEW, 1973. This eight-page leaflet describes federal laws and regulations which prohibit sex discrimination as of 1973. Includes a list of ten regional Offices for Civil Rights.

LEGAL MANDATES FOR SCHOOLS

Dunkle, Margaret, and Sandler, Bernice. *Sex Discrimination against Students: Implications of Title IX.* Washington: Project on the Status and Education of Women, 1974. Explains each section of the law, piece by piece and includes a summary of developments since Title IX regulations became effective. Addendum dated November 1975.

Inequality in Education/Sex Discrimination (October 18, 1974). This special issue contains six readable articles on the law prohibiting discrimination in education.

Pearson, Jessica. *Digest of Federal Laws: Equal Rights for Women in Education.* Denver: Education Commission of the States, 1975. This digest from the Equal Rights for Women in Education Project is currently unavailable, but a revision is forthcoming.

———. *Equal Rights for Women in Education: A Handbook of State Laws and Policies Affecting Equal Rights for Women in Education.* Denver: Education Commission of the States, 1975. State-by-state summaries of labor laws, fair employment practices legislation, anti-discrimination agencies, elementary and secondary level education policies and other areas of concern for women in education.

Raffel, Norma. *The Enforcement of Federal Laws and Regulations Prohibiting Sex Discrimination.* Washington: Women's Equity Action League, 1975. Examines major federal laws and regulations. Evaluates policy and enforcement, discusses problems and makes recommendations.

Resource Center on Sex Roles in Education. tion. *Combatting Discrimination in the Schools.* Washington: National Education Association, 1973. Booklet describes major laws which prohibit discrimination, includes an outline for identifying racial and sex discrimination in schools and suggestions for filing complaints.

Sandler, Bernice. *Sex Discrimination, Educational Institutions and the Law: A New Issue on Campus.* Washington: Project on the Status and Education of Women, 1973. This reprint from the *Journal of Law and Education* [2 (October 1973):613-635] summarizes the laws covering sex discrimination in education and analyzes the issues involved. U. S. Department of Health, Education and Welfare, Office for Civil Rights. *Final Title IX Regulation Implementing Education Amendments of 1972 Prohibiting Sex Discrimination in Education.* Washington: U. S. Department of HEW, 1975. This copy of the complete regulation includes a statement by Secretary Weinberger which discusses major issues of the law and other helpful information.

STRATEGIES FOR CHANGE Strategies for Change is divided into two sections. The first includes how-to reports from school districts which have made effective studies of their institutions, pinpointing areas of discrimination and implementing the necessary changes. Also listed are a number of programs and guidelines developed by research institutions to help in implementing Title IX. These serve as models. The second section provides a number of resources and syllabi for inservice education which, though not legally mandated, is an essential component of nonsexist education.

MODELS

American Association of School Administrators. The Association has three pamphlets in its Executive Handbook Series that are of interest: *Sex Equality in Educational Administration,* VII (1975); *Sex Equality in Educational Materials,* IV (1974); *Sex Equality in School,* V (1975).

Ann Arbor NOW, Committee to Eliminate Sex Discrimination in the Public Schools. *An Action Proposal to Eliminate Sex Discrimination in the Ann Arbor Public Schools.* Pittsburgh: KNOW, 1972.

Berkeley Unified School District, Women's Task Force. *In-Progress Report to the Board of Education.* Berkeley: Women's Task Force, 1972. Report includes statements of curricular, counseling, hiring and promotion problems, provides solutions to the problems and suggests areas of community involvement. Contains specific examples throughout.

Bostick, Nan; Kaspar, Patricia; and Sallan, Nancy. *How to Deal with Sex-Role Stereotyping—At a School Board Meeting—In a Workshop—In the Classroom.* Cupertino, Cal.: Choice for Tomorrow, 1976. This booklet provides step-by-step suggestions for positive action in countering sex stereotyping in schools, including classroom activities for grades K to six. Appendices provide useful recommendations, bibliography and checklists help evaluate sexism in reading materials.

Boulder NOW, Education Task Force. *Sex-Role Stereotyping in the Boulder Schools.* 1974. Available from Sharon L. Menard. This report on sex-role stereotyping within the curriculum and athletic programs of the Boulder schools includes recommendations for positive action.

Citizens' Advisory Council on the Status of Women. *Need for Studies of Sex Discrimination in Public Schools.* Washington: U.S. Department of Labor, 1972. This revised overview provides suggestions to assist organizations planning to review a school system. Appendices include selected bibliography.

ohen, M. *Stop Sex Role Stereotypes in Elementary Education: A Handbook for Parents and Teachers.* Hartford: Connecticut Public Interest Research Group, 1974. Provides ways to identify and combat sex-role stereotyping in curricula, teaching methods, administration policies and parent-teacher-child relations; suggests alternative materials and methods.

Committee on the Role and Image of Women. *Guidelines on Women's Roles.* Urbana: National Council of Teachers of English. NCTE has a *Guidelines* series which includes the following titles: *Guidelines for Confronting Attitudes that Penalize Women* (1973), *Guidelines for Combating Sexism in Language* (1974), *Guidelines for Publications* (1973) and *Guidelines for Women's Studies, Grades 1-12* (1974). All of these pamphlets are free.

Dallas Women's Coalition. *A Study of Sex Discrimination in the Dallas Independent School District.* This study, originally done in 1973, is being revised. Contact Jeanne Ford, Women's Center, University of Texas, Arlington, TX 76019.

Dayton Public Schools, Women's Rights Committee. *The Time Is Now* and *Choices.* Dayton: Public Schools, 1973. *The Time Is Now* is a study of employment practices and affirmative action recommendations. *Choices* examines sex bias and stereotyping in curricular and extracurricular activities in Dayton schools.

Federbush, Marcia. *Let Them Aspire: A Plea and Proposal for Equality of Opportunity for Males and Females in the Ann Arbor Public Schools.* Pittsburgh: KNOW, 1971. This study of sex-role stereotyping and discrimination in all areas of the Ann Arbor schools includes recommendations for action.

Harrison, Barbara. *Unlearning the Lie:*
Sexism in Schools. New York: Liveright, 1973. A personal account of the work of a group of Brooklyn parents who challenged the sexism in their children's classrooms.

Hawaii Task Force on Sex Bias in Education. *Report on Sex Bias in the Public Schools of Hawaii.* 1975. Available from Norma Titcomb. Detailed study of sex-role stereotyping and discrimination in all areas of Hawaii public schools; includes recommendations.

Institute for Educational Leadership. *Handbook on How to End Sexism in Your Schools.* Washington: Institute for Educational Leadership, George Washington University, 1975. Provides step-by-step procedures for evaluating sexism in schools and filing complaints. Two model programs are summarized.

Kalamazoo Public Schools, Committee to Study Sex Discrimination. Kalamazoo was one of the first systems to do a thorough self-evaluation, then recommend and implement a program for combatting sex discrimination. They have published a number of their reports, guidelines and recommendations, including *Report of the Task Force on Student Oriented Concerns, Recommendations for Eliminating Sex Discrimination in the Reading Program, Guidelines for the Evaluation of Print and Nonprint Materials, Sex Discrimination and Stereotyping in Music, Recommendations for Eliminating Discrimination in the Instructional Program.* Other Kalamazoo publications are listed in the appropriate sections of *Feminist Resources.* Write for a complete list of publications.

Kunkel, G. *Eliminating Sexism from the Public Schools of Washington State.* Seattle: Ad-hoc Committee for Women and Girls in Education, 1973. This 16-page guide includes an outline of the laws and regulations, information on career education, sexism in curriculum and counseling as well as recommendations for change.

Lexington Citizens' Advisory Committee on Educational Opportunities for Girls and Boys. *Sex Inequality in Lexington's Schools.* 1975. Available from Lexington School Committee. A study of sexism in employment practices, curriculum, teaching materials, counseling, sports and attitudes; includes recommendations.

Michigan State Department of Education. *Guidelines for Eliminating and Preventing Sex Discrimination.* Lansing: Office of Equal Educational Opportunity, 1976. Suggestions for specific actions to be taken in order to eliminate sex discrimination in curriculum, policy making and employment at all levels.

Minnesota State Department of Education, Sex Bias Task Force. *Report to the Minnesota State Board of Education.* St. Paul: Department of Education, 1974. This study includes a summary of anti-discrimination laws and regulations; recommendations on employment along with a model affirmative action program; examination of extracurricular athletics: suggestions for curriculum improvement, preservice and inservice training. Appendix provides background and supplementary information.

Nassau-Suffolk Council of Administrative Women in Education. *Guidelines for the Implementation of Title IX.* Oakdale, N.Y.: SCOPE, 1976. These guidelines help to clarify the subtleties and complexities of Title IX and to encourage investigation of sexist practices in an effort to seek positive change.

Pennsylvanians for Women's Rights. *Self-Study Guide to Sexism in Schools.* Harrisburg: Department of Education, 1973. A 22-page guide for Pennsyl-

vanians who want to know where to start in eradicating sexism from their schools. A model organizing tool for community and state-wide groups.

Project on the Status and Education of Women. *Partial List of Actions Institutions Must Take under Title IX.* Washington: Project on the Status and Education of Women, 1975. Explication of specific actions to fill some of the requirements of Title IX.

Raffel, Norma. *School Self-Evaluation under Title IX.* Washington: Women's Equity Action League.

Resource Center on Sex Roles in Education. *Complying with Title IX—A Resource Kit.* Washington: Women's Program Staff, U. S. Office of Education, 1976. A kit of technical assistance materials for the implementation of Title IX includes the following:

Equal Opportunity—A Fundamental American Right. This introductory pamphlet establishes a context for understanding Title IX.

Why Title IX? This booklet reviews some research evidence of sex discrimination in those areas covered by Title IX and discusses the possible implications of such discrimination.

Title IX of the Education Amendments of 1972. This detailed, pocket-size summary of the Regulation is intended to be used for easy reference.

Identifying Discrimination: A Review of Federal Antidiscrimination Laws and Selected Case Examples.

Complying with Title IX: The First Twelve Months. This booklet outlines the five required procedures that must be completed by July 21, 1976 and gives step-by-step aids for implementation.

Complying with Title IX: Implementing Institutional Self-Evaluation. This 142-page manual is organized into sections according to the substantive requirements of the Regulation. Each section contains a citation, a discussion of issues relating to compliance, specific data and questions for use in determining compliance and procedural checklists to assist in conducting the evaluation.

Title IX: Selected Resources. This is an annotated list of summaries, analyses, guidelines and other materials on Title IX.

Equal Educational Opportunity and Equal Employment Opportunity. These two posters outline the rights of students and employees to equal opportunity without regard to race or sex.

Rothchild, Nina. *Sexism in Schools: A Handbook for Action.* Available from Nina Rothchild. By a school board member, feminist and mother, this book is a practical guide for those who need to know how and where to start challenging school sexism. Includes bibliography and legal information.

Timpano, Doris M. *Is Your School District in Compliance with Title IX?* New York: Career Women in Education, 1975. This brief pamphlet is a series of checklists to guide and gauge a school's compliance with Title IX.

Walker, Jacqueline. *A Model Affirmative Action Plan for School and Classroom Practices.* New Brunswick: Training Institute for Sex Desegregation of the Public Schools, Douglass College, 1976. Includes guidelines for conducting a school self-evaluation.

INSERVICE EDUCATION

Cornelia Wheadon Task Force on the Socialization of Children. *Growing Up Human: A Four-Session Course on Sex-Role Stereotyping.* Boston: Unitarian Universalist Women's Federation, n.d. The four sessions include: introduction and sexism in children's books; toys,

games, imaginative play; sex-role stereotyping in schools; TV.

Froschl, Merle; Howe, Florence; and Kaylen, Sharon. *Women's Studies for Teachers and Administrators: A Packet of Inservice Materials.* Old Westbury: The Feminist Press, 1975. Product of a nation-wide conference, this packet provides materials necessary for organizing inservice education aimed at eliminating sexism in the schools. Four major components organize the packet: an hour-long cassette of speeches of four feminist educators, model inservice course syllabi, samples of curriculum materials produced by teachers in inservice courses and a descriptive list of key resource groups.

Golden, Gloria, and Hunter, Lisa. *In all Fairness: A Handbook on Sex Role Bias in Schools.* San Francisco: Far West Laboratory, 1974. This booklet and the films which accompany it are designed to help teachers become aware of what sex-role stereotyping is. The handbook suggests classroom activities and discussion questions and provides factual information about sex differences.

Howard, Suzanne. *Liberating Our Children Ourselves.* Washington: American Association of University Women, 1975. A handbook of women's studies course materials for teacher educators, this is a valuable resource for inservice education.

National Education Association. *The Labels and Reinforcement of Sex Role Stereotyping.* Two full-color filmstrips (with 33 1/3 rpm sound narration) which can form the core of an inservice course or workshop, or be used as a supplement.

———. *Sex Role Stereotyping Edupak.* Washington: National Education Association, n.d. This multi-media kit includes all of NEA's resources on sex-role stereotyping and discrimination in schools.

Nickerson, Eileen T. et al. *Intervention*

23

Strategies for Changing Sex Role Stereotypes: A Procedural Guide. Dubuque: Kendall/Hunt, 1975. Written and oral awareness exercises with a programmed series of activities make this a valuable text for inservice education.

Resnik, Gail M. *Challenging Sex Discrimination: Training Modules.* Ann Arbor: Women's Commission, School of Education, University of Michigan, 1975. Available from Ulrich's Book Store.

Inservice kit for combatting sex discrimination in education, contains tests, exercises, bibliography. Useful for teachers of all levels as well as other education staff and community groups.

Strategies to Counteract Sex Role Stereotyping in the Elementary School. Available from Resource Options. A video documentary of actual classroom strategies conducted by a multi-ethnic group of teachers. Available for sale or rent.

Preschool and Elementary Education

READINGS The readings for the elementary school teacher include lists of annotated bibliographies of nonsexist readings for children as well as general materials to aid in the understanding of sex-role stereotypes and bias-free teaching.

NONSEXIST BOOKLISTS

Adell, Judith, and Klein, Hilary D. *A Guide to Nonsexist Children's Books.* Chicago: Academy Press, 1976. A 149-page annotated bibliography of fiction and nonfiction for preschool through twelfth grade, with an introduction by Alan Alda.

American Association of University Women. *Books with Options.* 1976. Available from A. C. Simmons. This is an annotated bibliography of nonsexist books for children which provide strong role models without regard to sex or social situation.

Boston Area Women in Libraries. *Tea and Muskets.* Somerville: Boston Area Women in Libraries, 1976. Annotated bibliography of children's books that covers fictional biographies and stories of the colonial period. Includes both positive and negative recommendations.

Davis, Enid. *156 Good Books for Girls.* Available from Enid Davis. Annotated list of fiction and nonfiction with positive images of girls for ages four to fourteen.

———. *The Liberty Cap: A Bimonthly Journal of Recently Published Non-stereotyped Children's Books and Resources.* December 1974-December 1976. Although this periodical ceased publication in December 1976, the issues in its history chronicle the developments in nonstereotyped books for children. Academy Press will publish the complete set in book form.

Education Task Force, Project Woman. *Books for Free Children.* Springfield, Ohio: Project Woman, 1975. Annotated bibliography of a wide range of nonsexist children's books. Includes fiction, poetry and biographies of contemporary and historical figures.

Feminists on Children's Media. *Little Miss Muffet Fights Back.* New York: Feminists on Children's Media, 1974. Available from Feminist Book Mart. The revised edition of this classic study is a 64-page annotated list of recommended nonsexist books about girls for young readers.

Kalamazoo Public Schools. *180 Plus: A Framework for Nonstereotyped Human Roles in Elementary Media Center Materials.* Kalamazoo: Kalamazoo Public Schools, 1976. A list of more than 180 nonsexist books, records and materials for the elementary school media center. Briefly annotated.

Stavn, Diane Gersoni. "Reducing the 'Miss Muffet' Syndrome: An Annotated Bibliography." *School Library Journal* 19 (January 1972):32-35. Nonsexist children's books, arranged by reading level.

GENERAL READINGS

Childhood Education/Overcoming Sex-Role Stereotypes (February 1976). This special issue of the *Journal of the Association for Childhood Education International* contains articles that describe the research on ascribed and biological sex differences between girls and boys. The suggestions for eliminating stereotyped behavior in the classroom will prove useful to parents, students and teachers.

Eaton, C., and Jacobs, C. *Sexism in the Elementary School.* Washington: Resource Center on Sex Roles in Education, 1972. Originally appearing in *Today's Education,* this article documents the sexist messages children receive in school and includes a checklist for analyzing sexism in school books.

Elementary English/Women and Girls (October 1973). This special issue deals specifically with sexism in children's literature and sex-role stereotypes in children's writing. Includes interviews with authors of children's books.

Gardner, Jo-Ann et al. *Sesame Street and Sex-Role Stereotypes.* Pittsburgh: KNOW, 1970. Analysis of the popular children's TV show.

Jameson, Dee Dee, and Grams, Armis. "Changing Roles for Women and Men." *Childhood Education* 49 (January 1973): 184-190.

Klapper, Zelda S. "The Impact of the Women's Movement on Child Development Books." *American Journal of Orthopsychiatry* 41 (October 1971): 725-732. Incisive analysis of feminist challenges to the traditional assumptions behind child development theories that enforce rigid sex-role socialization.

MacEwan, Phyllis. *Liberating Young Children from Sex Roles.* Somerville: New England Free Press, 1972. An excellent analysis of the teacher's role in intervention in the sex-typed behavior of young children. Emphasis is on teacher behavior.

Miles, Betty. *Channeling Children: Sex Stereotyping in Prime-Time TV.* Princeton: Women on Words and Images, 1975. An analysis of 20 TV shows which documents the extent of sex stereotyping in popular television.

——. "Women's Liberation Comes to Class." *Scholastic Teacher/Elementary Edition* (November 1971):9-10.

Moberg, Verne. *A Child's Right to Equal Reading: Exercises in the Liberation of Children's Books from the Limitations of Sexual Stereotypes.* Old Westbury: The Feminist Press, 1972. Includes a model for a community workshop on children's books, with suggestions for examining stereotype patterns.

Sadker, Myra, and Sadker, David. "Sexual Discrimination in the Elementary School." *National Elementary Principal* (October 1972):41-45.

Schoettler, Jim. "Male, Damn It." *Saturday Review: Education* 1 (April 1973): 13. This short article by a first-grade teacher tells of his attempt to eradicate sexism in his classroom.

Shargel, Susan, and Kane, Irene. *We Can Change It!* San Francisco: Change for Children, 1974. This text suggests ways of integrating nonsexist books into all phases of classroom and family life. Includes an annotated bibliography of nonsexist, nonracist children's books.

Sprung, Barbara. *Nonsexist Education for Young Children: A Practical Guide.* New York: The Women's Action Alliance, 1975. This book raises important questions about stereotyping for people who are just beginning to question male/female sex roles as well as those who are already working to change them. Provides concrete suggestions for implementing change and an annotated bibliography and resource list of materials, organizations and publications.

Women's Action Alliance. *A Model for Nonsexist Child Development: A Pre-School Program.* New York: Women's Action Alliance, 1975. This 32-page booklet describes the organizations's extensive preschool program and contains an annotated bibliography. Provides an excellent step-by-step model for establishing similar activities.

CURRICULUM The elementary school curriculum has been divided into two sections. In the first are lesson plans, books, articles and entire units to help in planning a nonsexist curriculum. The second section contains nonprint materials—photos, posters, records—for use in the classroom.

Abt Associates. *Career Education Activities for Subject Area Teachers.* Cambridge: Abt Associates, 1975. This set of nonsexist lesson sheets and activities on career education are designed to be integrated into the existing core curriculum, grades one to six.

Burt, Olive W. *Black Women of Valor.* New York: Julian Messner, 1974. Brief, easy-to-read biographies of Juliette Derricotte, Maggie Mitchell Walker, Ida Wells Barnett and Septima Poinsette Clarke. Recommended for grades four and up.

Career Futures, Inc. *Children's Dictionary of Occupations.* Philadelphia: Career Futures.

Free to Be You and Me. Available from Free to Be Foundation. Available as an illustrated hardcover or paperback (New York: McGraw-Hill, 1974) as well as the now-classic record (Bell Records). Delightful stories and songs for and about children who challenge sex roles.

Froschl, Merle, ed. *Storypack.* Old Westbury: The Feminist Press, 1974. Five separate stories in booklet form that deal with children's feelings about divorce, about being called a sissy, about their bodies and masturbation, about being heroes and about sex roles. A guide for teachers and parents is included.

Goldreich, Gloria, and Goldreich, Esther. *What Can She Be? A Lawyer/Veterinarian/Newscaster/Architect/Musician/ Police Officer.* New York: Lothrop, Lee

and Shepard. These six books give a realistic introduction to careers and depict women in a variety of family situations who work and are happy with their lives. Includes pictures of women involved in nontraditional careers.

Gould, Lois. "X: A Fabulous Child's Story." *Ms.* (December 1972):74-77. This ingenious story is an excellent tool for consciousness-raising with children of all ages. "X," a child whose gender is not known, is brought up to explore all kinds of games and develop all kinds of skills which cause havoc among family, friends and teachers.

Groves, Susan et al. *Women's Studies Program.* Berkeley: Berkeley Unified School District, n.d. A wealth of nonsexist curricular materials designed for early childhood through grade six has been developed by the Women's Studies Program, which is an integral part of the Berkeley Public Schools. Write for their brochure which describes the materials (lessons and activities, units, media and library materials) in detail.

Landau, Elaine. *Hidden Heroines: Women in American History.* New York: Julian Messner, 1975. Written for grades four to seven, this book accurately portrays women's role in America's history from the colonies through the passage of the 19th amendment.

Levenson, Dorothy. *Women of the West.* New York: Franklin Watts, 1973. The title is somewhat misleading as the book deals with women of the nineteenth century as well as with women of the west. Amply illustrated with reproductions of old political cartoons, advertisements, illustrations and photographs, it contains much useful and interesting information. Recommended for upper elementary school students.

Olsen, Laurie, ed. *Nonsexist Curricular Materials for Elementary Schools.* Old Westbury: The Feminist Press, 1977. This packet of materials for the teacher and student is being revised. The new edition will include detailed suggestions for recognizing sexism, model curricular units, a student workbook, readings, a bibliography of available histories and biographies and a nonsexist fiction list.

Project Equality. *Occupation Simulation Packets.* Seattle: The Highline School District, 1975. Packets aid students to identify and apply their skills in a simulated work experience designed to reduce sex-role stereotyping. Activities are focused on a single skill which is already possessed by the student, such as crawling and/or squatting, color discrimination, measuring.

——. *The Yellow Blue and Red Book.* Seattle: The Highline School District, 1975. A collection of short-term activities designed to look at traditional sex-role stereotyping with elementary students.

Racism and Sexism Resource Center for Educators. *Sexism, Racism and Other Isms: Hidden Messages in Children's Stories.* New York: Racism and Sexism Resource Center for Educators, n.d. A lesson plan for grades five and up, which teaches how to spot hidden messages in the simplest of stories. Uses *The Princess and the Pea* to open discussion.

Resource Center on Sex Roles in Education. *Today's Changing Roles: An Ap-* *proach to Nonsexist Teaching.* Washington: Resource Center on Sex Roles in Education, 1974. This 108-page book contains lesson plans that clearly define concepts and goals as well as list the materials that will be necessary for students to explore the issue of sex-role stereotyping on a personal level. Helps identify sex roles in magazines, texts and on television.

Stevenson, Janet. *Women's Rights.* New York: Franklin Watts, 1972. A well-illustrated, clearly-written book about the struggle of women to gain full rights as citizens in this country. The book examines and evaluates the history of the women's movement past and present. Some interesting prints and photographs are included. Recommended for upper elementary readers.

Wayne, Bennett. *Women Who Dared to Be Different.* Champaign: Garrard, 1973. Easy-to-read short biographies of Annie Oakley, Maria Mitchell, Nellie Bly and Amelia Earhart. Includes photos, with brief commentaries, of other women in the same or related fields.

——. *Women with a Cause.* Champaign: Garrard.

——. *Four Women of Courage.* Champaign: Garrard.

The Women's Kit . . . and More. *Nonsexist Curricular Materials for Elementary Schools.* Toronto: The Women's Kit . . . and More, Ontario Institute for Studies in Education, 1974. A series of projects and discussion starters on sex-role stereotyping in texts and the commercial media. The section on women and Canadian history provides a good curricular model.

NONPRINT CURRICULAR MATERIALS

The American Women's Role—Yesterday and Today. Elgin: David C. Cook. Sixteen 12" x 17" color pictures that dramatize the past achievements of women. The pictures are accompanied by a 32-page manual.

Bodies. Edison: Childcraft. Plywood-backed, 25-piece puzzle depicting nude white male and black female children.

Feminist Resources for Equal Education. *Women in Nontraditional Roles.* Framingham: Feminist Resources for Equal Education. Two sets each contain eight 8½" x 11" photographs: Set #1, Community Helpers; Set #2, Professional Women.

Free to Be You and Me. New York: McGraw-Hill Film Division, 1976. A new 16 mm film of the one-hour TV telecast as well as four classroom learning modules.

Home and Family. Paoli, Pa.: Instructo. Twenty-four pictures of families which include representations of family members of various age groups and of many different racial groups.

Hurray for Captain Jane. Caedmon Records. 1975. Nonsexist stories read by Tammy Grimes.

Judy Puzzles. This company produces a variety of nonsexist, nonracist puzzles: *Occupations Puzzles.* Thirteen wooden puzzles representing women and minorities in a variety of roles. *The City.* A 2' x 3', 20-piece "floor puzzle" showing people working and going about their daily chores in a big city. *The Park.* Another "floor puzzle" depicting women and men, some in nontraditional roles, in a park setting.

Kane, Irene. *Women at Work.* San Francisco: Change for Children, 1974. This packet includes fifteen 8" x 10" photo-reproductions of women of different ages and ethnic backgrounds working in nontraditional jobs. An effective visual resource.

Living Together in America. Elgin: David C. Cook. Twenty 12" x 17" color pictures of various ethnic groups in American society.

Mothers Do many Kinds of Work. Oakland: Scott, Foresman. Free posters.

National Education Association. *Blue Is for Sky, Pink Is for Watermelon.* Washington: NEA. Cassette and discussion questions. Eve Merriam reads five selections from her anti-sexist poems.

Our Story: Women Today and Yesterday. Chicago: Science Research Associates. Unit Box on Women.

Project Equality. *Many Thousand Words— Work Pictures.* Seattle: The Highline School District, 1975. This collection of 8" x 10" laminated, black-and-white pictures shows that all people (girls and boys, women and men) use their skills and abilities to do a variety of jobs—at home, at school, in the community.

Racism and Sexism Resource Center for Educators. *Picture-Pac Activity on Sexism.* New York: Racism and Sexism Resource Center for Educators, n.d. Ten photos to be examined by small groups of students who discuss which are, and which are not, sexist. Recommended for grades five and up.

Robot. Pasadena: Fundamentals. An alternative to "Old Maid," this nonsexist card game portrays women and men in almost identical work roles and clothing.

Women's Action Alliance. This group has developed a variety of nonprint materials for use in the early childhood and elementary classroom. Some are now produced by commercial companies, all materials are available through the Women's Action Alliance:

Our Helpers. Milton Bradley. Twelve stand-up cardboard figures show men and women in a variety of jobs in the community. Includes teacher's guide.

My Family. Milton Bradley. Twelve

stand-up cardboard figures allow children to dramatize a variety of family situations. Figures represent black and white people of different ages. Included are suggestions for using the figures in classroom situations.

People at Work. Instructo/McGraw-Hill. Twenty-four nonsexist, multi-racial, 8" x 11" photographs of women and a few men involved in nontraditional careers. Includes a teacher's guide for use with the visual aids.

Community Careers. Instructo/McGraw-Hill. Flannel board plus figures (women and men), props (fire hydrant, mailbox, etc.) and name cards (police officer, construction worker, etc.) for students to mix and match and develop an understanding that both women and men do important jobs of all kinds in the community.

Play Scenes Lotto. Milton-Bradley. Multi-racial, nonsexist game showing possible active roles for boys and girls playing together.

Pictures of Men in Nurturing Roles. Eight 8" x 10" photographs that show girls and boys in active play and men working closely with them in nurturing roles.

Secondary Education

READINGS The readings for the teacher in this section include the few available volumes of course outlines and syllabi, as well as articles on the teaching of women's studies in high school. General information of interest to all teachers can be found in the Overview (see Basic Readings).

Ahlum, Carol, and Fralley, Jacqueline. "Feminist Studies." *Today's Education* 61 (December 1972):26. Discussion of curriculum materials for high school women's studies.

——, comps. *High School Feminist Studies,* ed. Florence Howe. Old Westbury: The Feminist Press, 1975. This volume contains the work of 23 of the nation's pioneers in high school women's studies. The high school course syllabi are divided into three sections: history, literature and interdisciplinary. Also included is "Women in the High School Curriculum," an analysis of the treatment of women in U. S. history and English literature texts.

California Council for the Social Studies Review/Women in the Social Studies (Fall 1972). This special issue is a collection of essays on methods and curriculum for teaching about women in high school social studies classes.

Cebik, L. B. "Women's Studies and Home Economics." *Journal of Home Economics* 67 (January 1975):27-30.

Clapp, Ouida H., ed. *Classroom Practices in Teaching English, 1976-77.* Urbana: National Council of Teachers of English, forthcoming. The more than 20 articles in this collection provide practical ideas and strategies for helping students develop an awareness of the effects of sexism as they explore literature. Includes a bibliography for teaching about women in literature.

Collins, J. A. "Reflective Examination of the Feminine Role: Teaching Strategies." *The High School Journal* 58 (March 1975):259-273.

Emma Willard Task Force on Education. *Sexism in Education.* Minneapolis: Emma Willard Task Force on Education, 1973. This book of materials, now in its third edition, includes bibliographies, consciousness-raising exercises for teachers and students, a checklist for evaluating sexism in instructional materials and a game.for counselors to use with students about career aspirations and sex roles.

Feminists Northwest. *Again at the Looking Glass.* Seattle: Feminists Northwest, 1975. These materials were developed to encourage teachers and students to overcome the sexism often present in the language arts curriculum. A good resource for teachers, it includes suggestions for activities and discussions, as well as bibliographies for sexist language, autobiography, nonsexist literature and sexism in the media.

Fowler, Lois Josephs. "Sirens and Seeresses: Women in Literature and the High School Curriculum." *English Journal* 62 (November 1973):1123-1126. A description of the methods teachers can use to raise issues related to women's lives, with suggestions for teaching electives designed to explore the role of women in literature.

Grambs, Jean Dresden, ed. *Teaching about Women in the Social Studies: Concepts, Methods and Materials.* Arlington: National Council for the Social Studies, 1976. A resource book for social studies teachers who want to avoid sexism and make women a viable part of the study of history. Each chapter presents basic concepts to help teachers analyze and revise their current teaching as well as build new units and courses. Resources and bibliographies are included.

Gates, Barbara; Klaw, Susan; and Reich, Adria. *The Group School Curriculum* (tentative title). Old Westbury: The Feminist Press, forthcoming. This comprehensive women's studies curriculum has been developed and taught at The Group School, an alternative high school for working-class youth in Cambridge, Massachusetts. The curriculum is divided into nine thematic units, which range from "Messages from Society," to "Women and Work." Throughout, suggestions are made on "how to," as well as "what to" teach.

Kotzin, Miriam. "Women, like Blacks and Orientals, Are all Different: A Resource Unit on Women." *Media and Methods* 8 (March 1972):18-22.

Lane, M. T. "Women's Studies in the University Curriculum." *The High School Journal* 59 (October 1975):1-8.

No More Teachers' Dirty Looks (Summer 1973) Available from BARTOC. This special issue is an illustrated guide to teaching materials on women's studies—articles that are easy to obtain and duplicate for the classroom. In general, this magazine regularly features articles on sexism in education and on women's studies.

Olejniczak, Gabrielle. "Women's Studies in the Junior High School." ERIC/ Chess. Description of a nine-week course, "Woman: Her Image and Her Role," taught at the Cherry Creek, Colorado, middle school. Included is a discussion on the introduction of women's studies into the curriculum.

Rosenfelt, Deborah Silverton, ed. *Strong Women.* Old Westbury: The Feminist Press, 1976. More than 100 widely available paperbacks are annotated in this bibliography of literature for the high school classroom. Includes sections on anthologies, autobiography, biography, drama, novels, short stories and poetry, as well as a cross-topical index. Illustrated with photographs of women writers—all of which will help to supplement the traditional male bias of contemporary textbooks.

Rowley-Rotunno, V., and Dobkin, W. S., "Curriculum Considerations and Learning Strategies in the Teaching of Women's Studies." *The High School Journal* 57 (February 1974):182-189.

Stanford, Gene, and Stanford, Barbara. "I Am Woman, You Are Man: A Mini-Course in Sexual Identity." *Scholastic Teacher* (October 1972):52-55. Essay about a course taught by the authors in a variety of situations; includes bibliography.

Trecker, Janice Law. "Teaching the Role of Women in American History; with Suggested Teaching Strategies by E. O. Pearson." *National Council for the Social Studies Yearbook* 43 (1973): 278-297.

Valiant, Sharon. *People* Working (*Especially Women).* New Brunswick: Training Institute for Sex Desegregation of the Public Schools, 1976. This resource book is mainly bibliography, but also contains some activities and ideas for the classroom about women working, past and present.

Wells, Nancy. "Women in American Literature." *English Journal* 62 (November 1973):1159-1161. Description of a modular course, taught at San Pedro High School, using examples from literature to introduce the concept of alternative choices for women in the American culture.

Wolfson, Sharon. "Twelve and Turned On." *Women: A Journal of Liberation* 1 (Winter 1970):38-39. Description of a course taught to women students in a junior high school.

Women in Literature Collective. *Women and Literature: An Annotated Bibliography of Women Writers.* Cambridge: Women in Literature Collective, 1976.

This annotated bibliography is now in its third edition and has grown enormously—both in size and in scope. Sections on American and British writers, from the nineteenth century to the present, comprise more than one-half the book. An international section includes women writers from 16 countries. Biographical information is available for all major authors. Subject and author indexes are included.

CURRICULUM The high school curriculum has been divided into three areas: Social Studies, Literature and Interdisciplinary. The categories necessarily overlap, since by their very definition, all high school women's studies courses are interdisciplinary in nature. The Social Studies section contains much historical material along with information on the American woman's role in today's society; the Literature section has been kept small, in order not to duplicate the bibliography *Strong Women* (see Readings); the Interdisciplinary section covers the areas of health, family living and sex roles in general. Teachers should also refer to the Women's Movement section (see Overview/Basic Readings) for materials that would be appropriate as classroom texts. Multi-media curricular materials have been grouped together at the end of each subject category.

SOCIAL STUDIES

The American Family: Life Styles in a Changing Society. Columbus: Xerox Education Publications, 1975. This paperback explores the ways in which the American family is changing, focusing on the characteristics and values of the middle-class American family. There is a discussion of alternatives to the traditional family. Separate teaching guide.

American Women. New York: Cambridge Book Company, 1973. A series of four books depicting the changing roles of women: *Their Image (1900's-1930's), Transition Period (1930's-1970's), Emancipation and Radicalism (1950's-1970's), Today (1960's-1970's).*

Committee to Study Sex Discrimination, Kalamazoo Public Schools. *Famous American Women.* Kalamazoo Public Schools, 1973. Brief biographies of 125 American women who have made significant contributions to art and literature, athletics, performing arts, science, education, professions, politics, women's rights and humanity.

———. *Notable Women of Science.* Kalamazoo: Kalamazoo Public Schools, 1974. An answer to queries for information on women in science—an eight-page listing subdivided into 15 scientific fields. Bibliography included.

———. *Women in Art.* Kalamazoo: Kalamazoo Public Schools, 1975. A listing of 80 slides available from the Kalamazoo Art Center presenting works of women artists in the fields of graphics, painting, sculpture, photography and media. The brief biographies and comments regarding each artist's style make this good general reference material for students.

Belden, Jack. *Gold Flower's Story*. Somerville: New England Free Press. This vivid excerpt from *China Shakes the World* recounts a woman's struggle to change her life during the Chinese revolution.

The Black Scholar. This publication has produced three special issues (December 1971, March 1973, March 1975) containing articles on a variety of aspects of black women's experience.

Chapin, June R., and Branson, Margaret Stimman. *Women: The Majority-Minority*. Boston: Houghton-Mifflin, 1973. This paperback covers issues of the women's rights movement, including women and work, child care, marriage, legal equality, image of women in the mass media, sexism in education. Discussion questions, student activities and a bibliography are included.

Corrective Collective. *She Named It Canada*. Available from Hogtown Press. This pamphlet of cartoons is a people's history of Canada in which women are consistently present.

——. *Never Done: Three Centuries of Women's Work in Canada*. Toronto: Canadian Women's Educational Press.

Dubois, Ellen. *Struggling into Existence*. Somerville: New England Free Press. Article on Sarah and Angelina Grimké, ex-slaveholders from South Carolina who, in the mid-1830's, were the "midwives of the birth of American feminism."

Flexner, Eleanor. *Women's Rights—Unfinished Business*. 1971. Available from Public Affairs Pamphlet Series. Description of the ways in which "all women are not equally well off or equally satisfied."

Franki, M., and Hillstrom, J. *America's First Unfinished Revolution*. Detroit: News & Letters Committees, 1976. A pamphlet that counteracts the myths that have distorted America's revolutionary history. It tells the story of the workers, yeomen, blacks, Indians and women and makes the connection with the freedom movements of today.

Froines, Ann. *Women's Work Is Never Done*. Somerville: New England Free Press, 1972. A dramatic reading on the story of the work women have done throughout history.

Gould, Elsie M. *American Woman Today: Free or Frustrated?* Englewood Cliffs: Prentice-Hall, 1977. Part of the publisher's "Inquiry into Crucial American Problems" series, this paperback focuses on the role of women today. Includes chapters on: How It Used to Be, What Is the Status of Women Today, What Do Women Want, Men React and What Will the Future Bring. Includes discussion questions and a bibliography.

Grant, Anne. "Women's Liberation or Exploding the Fairy Princess Myth." *Scholastic Teacher/Junior, Senior High School Edition* (November 1971):6-11.

Greene, Felix. *Divorce Trial in China*. Somerville: New England Free Press. An excerpt from Greene's book on China that tells the story of women winning the right of divorce after the Chinese revolution.

Ingraham, Claire R., and Ingraham, Leonard W. *An Album of Women in American History*. New York: Franklin Watts, 1972. Designed primarily for high school students, this volume offers a variety of short biographical sketches and illustrations about women.

Jacobs, William Jay. *Women in American History*. Beverly Hills: Benziger, 1976.

This paperback provides a perspective on the history of women in the United States—outstanding women as well as those whose names are forgotten. Divided chronologically into three sections— From Plymouth to Fort Sumter (1620-1860), Beyond Appomattox (1860-1900) and The Twentieth-Century Women—each section includes original diaries and primary materials, pictures of women in art and questions for discussion.

Judd, Barbara, and Josephs, Daniel. *Women in the United States.* Glenview: Scott, Foresman, 1975. Part of the publisher's "Readings in American History" series, this paperback presents a comprehensive picture of women's roles. Divided into 14 topics, including Women on the Frontier, Women and Work, Hearth and Home, New Dilemmas for Women and The Nature of Woman. Discussion questions included.

Journal of Afro-American Issues/Black Women in America (Summer 1974).

Landau, Elaine. *Woman, Woman! Feminism in America.* New York: Julian Messner, 1974. This book describes the achievements of women in America's history, the stereotypes that limited their potential, the demands for full equality now and in the future. Includes chapters on health, life styles and minority women.

Langer, Elinor. *The Women of the Telephone Company.* Somerville: New England Free Press, 1970. A personal and vivid description and analysis of the work women do for the telephone company.

Lerner, Gerda. *The Woman in American History.* Reading, Mass.: Addison-Wesley, 1971. A good, basic, short readable history of women in America. Informative on black and working women.

McBee, Mary Louise, and Blake, Kathryn A. *The American Woman: Who Will*

She Be? Beverly Hills: Glencoe Press, 1974. Ten essays focus on the present status and future possibilities of women, covering a wide range of topics—history, adjustment and mental health, self-actualization, androgyny, life styles, occupations, new social structures, the media, government, politics and higher education. Discussion questions, suggested projects and selected readings are included.

Maupin, Joyce. *Working Women and Their Organizations: 150 Years of Struggle.* Berkeley: Union WAGE Educational Committee, 1974. This booklet outlines in detail how women organized, from the first women's strike in 1824 to drives and picket lines today.

———. *Labor Heroines—Ten Women Who Led the Struggle.* Berkeley: Union WAGE Educational Committee, 1975. An excellent companion piece to *Working Women and Their Organizations,* this booklet contains short biographies on such leaders as Sarah Bagley, Hannah O'Day, Rose Schneiderman, Mother Jones and Elizabeth Gurley Flynn.

Meltzer, Milton, ed. *Women of America.* New York: Thomas Y. Crowell. This series of biographies provides inspiring examples of women who have led active and purposeful lives and who have made major contributions to our society. Included are: Frances Wright, Fanny Kemble, Felisa Rincon de Gautier, Gertrude Stein, Abby Kelley Foster, Ida Tarbell, Mother Jones, Pearl Buck, Margaret Sanger, Emma Goldman, Lydia Maria Child, Marry Cassatt.

Millstein, Beth, and Bodin, Jeanne. *We, The American Women: A Documentary History.* New York: Jerome S. Ozer, 1975. A combination of narrative, historical documents and illustrations record the history of women's contributions to American life from the earliest settlements to the 1970's. An extensive bibliography follows each of the 12 chapters; a teacher's manual is available.

Osen, Lynn M. *Women in Mathematics.* Cambridge: The MIT Press, 1974. This 185-page book profiles the lives of women who have had an impact on the development of mathematical thought—from antiquity through the present.

O'Sullivan, Judith, and Galleck, Rosemary. *Workers and Allies: Female Participation in the American Trade Union Movement, 1824-1976.* Washington: Smithsonian Institution Press, 1975. This book traces 150 years of the history of labor through biographical sketches of the white and Third World women involved in the movement. A chronology, extensive biographies and a good selection of photographs make this a useful text.

Pollack, George, and Cutter, Charles L. *Women in American Life.* Columbus: Xerox Education Publications, 1976. Women are part of the history of our country, and this 48-page booklet documents it with diaries, writings and true-life stories of America's little-known women heroes. Also included is a look at the American woman's role today. Most appropriate for junior high school; a separate teaching guide is available.

Reid, Willie Mae. *Black Women's Struggle for Equality.* New York: Pathfinder Press, 1976. This new pamphlet contains contributions from Willie Mae Reid ("Changing Attitudes among Black Women"), Linda Jenness ("Black Women Fight Sterilization"), Cindy Jaquith ("Joanne Little's Victory") and Pat Wright ("Black Women and the ERA").

San Francisco Women's History Group. *What Have Women Done?* San Francisco: United Front Press, n.d. An excellent photo essay on the history of working women in the United States,

beginning with the colonial period, and including the story of slavery, the Lowell Mills, European immigrants, labor organizing, civil rights.

Scott, Anne F., ed. *The American Woman: Who Was She?* Englewood Cliffs: Prentice-Hall, 1971. A relatively easy text that presents a good basic review of the role of women in America.

———. *Women in American Life.* Boston: Houghton-Mifflin, 1970. Part of the publisher's "Life in America" series, this paperback contains selected readings— reproduced as they appeared in the original sources—that tell the story of women's changing roles and life styles. Beginning with Amerindian women, it ends with a new era of feminism. Questions for study and discussion are included.

Seifer, Nancy. *Absent from the Majority: Working Class Women in America.* New York: National Project on Ethnic America of the American Jewish Committee, 1973. Monograph on white ethnic women and the effects that social changes of the past 20 years have had on them. Suggests new social policy and includes recommendations for changes in the areas of work, education, family, community and society at large.

———. *Nobody Speaks for Me! Self-Portraits of American Working Class Women.* New York: Simon and Schuster, 1976. A collection of oral histories of ten women activists.

Smuts, Robert M. *Women and Work in America.* New York: Schocken Books, 1971. A comprehensive and definitive text that gives an accurate historical picture of women at work, paid and unpaid.

Stanton, Elizabeth Cady. *Seneca Falls Resolutions and Declaration of Sentiments.* Pittsburgh: KNOW. A reprint of the resolutions and declarations adopted at the first equal rights for women meeting in the United States on July 18-19, 1848.

Taylor, Kathryn. *Generations of Denial: Seventy-Five Short Biographies of Women in History.* New York: Times Change Press, 1972. Stories of women not found in traditional history books—a good supplement for junior and senior high school texts.

Vidal, Mirta. *Chicanas Speak Out—Women: New Voice of La Raza.* New York: Pathfinder Press, 1971. This article first appeared in the *International Socialist Review* and includes the major resolutions approved at the first national Chicana conference of Raza women. The article focuses on the results of the two largest workshops: "Sex and the Chicana" and "Marriage—Chicana Style."

Williams, Maxine, and Newman, Pamela. *Black Women's Liberation.* New York: Pathfinder Press, 1972. A pamphlet containing two articles: "Why Liberation Is Important to Black Women," by Maxine Williams, which looks at the real condition and history of the so-called dominant black woman; and "Take a Good Look at Our Problems," by Pamela Newman. Both articles originally appeared in *The Militant* in 1970.

Women at Work, Ontario, 1850-1930. Toronto: The Canadian Women's Educational Press.

Women's Liberation Center of Nassau County. *High School Speakers' Project: A Special Unit on Women for High School Classes.* Available from Barbara Sussman. This unit provides high school teachers and students with comprehensive materials for exploring many of the issues of the women's liberation movement.

Woodroofe, Debby. *Sisters in Struggle 1848-1920.* New York: Pathfinder Press, 1971. Pamphlet that comprehensively describes the struggle for women's suffrage—and the importance of women recovering their history.

SOCIAL STUDIES/MULTI-MEDIA

Aunit Molly Jackson. Rounder Records. Songs from the 1930's in Kentucky, sung by a union organizer and storyteller.

But the Women Rose: Voices of Women in American History. Folkways Records. These two volumes contain moving statements by women throughout American history, 1700's to the present; script included.

The Feminist Revolution/Pioneers in a Man's World. Documentary Photo Aids. Twenty-six 11" x 14" photo posters in black and white. Each poster provides explanation of social/political attitudes of the time. Teacher's guide with discussion questions for students is included.

Identity Female. New York: Dun-Donnelly, 1975. A modular multi-media women's studies program, that examines its subject from the viewpoint of different disciplines: anthropology, history, psychology, sociology, economics, law. Although advertised for use in high school through junior college, we recommend the materials for a younger audience. Particularly good for high school is the filmstrip which reviews 700 years of art by women.

Jackdaw Kits. New York: Grossman Publishers. These excellent kits contain primary source materials (letters, facsimiles of manuscripts, songs and pictures) not found in standard texts. They provide valuable references and teaching tools for the social studies classroom: *Women's Rights in the United States,* compiled by Mary Stetson Clarke; *Women in the American Revolution,* compiled by Carol Berkin; *Women in Revolt,* compiled by Judith Kazantzis.

Ms. America. Englewood Cliffs: Scholastic

Audio-Visual Center. Part of Scholastic's "American Adventures" filmstrip program, this is an excellent summary of women's role in America from the colonies to the present. Photographs, selections from diaries and other primary sources are included in the narrative.

The Negro Woman. Folkways Records. Documentary of the accomplishments of black women, including: Phyllis Wheatley, Sojourner Truth, Harriet Tubman, Frances Ellen Watkins Harper, Ida Wells Barnett, Mary Church Terrell, Mary McLeod Bethune.

Pioneer Women: Selections from Their Journals. Caedmon Records. Sandy Dennis and Eileen Heckart read moving selections that describe the experience of four pioneer women: a homesteader, an army wife, a missionary and a pioneer daughter.

Recovering Our Past: Part I, The Struggle for Women's Suffrage. The Feminist History Research Project. This research project has recorded hundreds of hours of oral history with participants in the women's movement at the beginning of the century. The first program, a 24-minute slide/tape presentation, combines the recorded voices of women who participated in the 72-year-long battle for the right to vote, with historical engravings and photographs.

Seneca Falls. Interact. This simulation of the first women's rights convention in July, 1848, recreates the activities of the convention, using historical documents.

The Silenced Majority. Media Plus. This five-part multi-media presentation on the status of women in the United States contains full-color filmstrips, records or cassettes, discussion guide, poster and stickers.

Songs of the Suffragettes. Folkways Records. A ballad documentary of the women's suffrage movement.

Watch Out Girlie: Women's Liberation Is Gonna Get Your Momma. University Christian Movement in New England. An effective slide show—four carousels and a tape—about the issues of the women's movement. The pop background music makes a humorous and moving introduction for feminist issues. Also available: a resource packet, "Women in the Struggle for Liberation."

Who Are These Mystery Women? Englewood Cliffs: Scholastic Magazines. An attractive poster with black-and-white photographs of women who should not remain a mystery.

Women: An American History. Encyclopaedia Britannica. Six filmstrips and cassettes, each one focusing on a particular era in women's history: Women of the New World, The Mill Girl and the Lady, The Fight for Equality, a Combination of Work and Hope, Beyond the Vote, The Modern Women's Movement. Photographs and narration are excellent; teacher's guide included.

Women Artists. New York: Harper and Row, 1976. This slide program grows out of years of intensive research by J. J. Wilson and Karen Petersen. The four programs—a total of 360 unique transparencies and notes—feature the long-ignored abilities and perspectives of more than 200 women artists. The four include: A Historical Survey (Early Middle Ages to 1900); The Twentieth Century; Third World; Images—Themes and Dreams. The authors have also written a book based on their research, entitled *Recognition and Reappraisal from the Early Middle Ages to the Twentieth Century.* New York: Harper Colophon, 1976.

Women in American History. Educational Activities. An excellent narrative and expressive and moving illustrations bring to life women in: The Colonies, After the

Revolution, Slavery and Sufferage, Reformers, The Artist, Crisis of Identity. Six filmstrips, plus cassettes or records; teacher's guides included.

The Women's Kit. Toronto: The Ontario Institute for Studies in Education. This multi-media kit about women and their socialization contains records, slides, articles, filmstrips, posters, photos, plays, newspapers, poems, drawings, stories, lists, booklets. Among its varied contents are 50 slides of work by contemporary Canadian women artists and a recorded interview with a militant suffragist.

Women's Work; America: 1620-1920. Schloat Productions. This historical survey of work in and out of the home presents a factual and meaningful view of events in America's past. Four filmstrips with records or cassettes.

The Work of the Women. Womenfolk Song Project. Songs reflect American women's experiences throughout history, including housework, mothering, the labor movement, suffrage, temperance. Teacher's guide and bibliography, suitable for a mini-course on Women in History, is included.

The Working Girl: Women's Songs from Mountains, Mines and Mills. Voyager Recordings. Lively and traditional Appalachian songs about women, featuring Kathy Kahn, author of *Hillbilly Women.*

LITERATURE

Folsom, Marcia McClintock, and Kirschner, Linda Heinlein. *By Women: An Anthology of Literature.* Boston: Houghton-Mifflin, 1976. A collection of short stories, poetry, drama and nonfiction organized into units arranged by genre as well as themes: Search for Self, In a Role, Breaking Free. This anthology, unlike standard high school texts, speaks to the creative energies of women over some 2500 years and reflects a variety of backgrounds, races and culture. The companion Instructor's Resource Book includes discussion questions, background information, suggested readings and a bibliography.

Hall, James; Jones, Nancy J.; and Sutherland, Janet, R. *Women: Portraits.* New York: McGraw-Hill, 1976. An anthology of literature that presents realistic portraits of women from differing cultures. It was designed not only to familiarize students with positive female characters, but to help them examine critically the unrealistic images of women found in the popular media. Three chapters are entitled: Women Becoming, Women Being and Women Stereotyped. Questions and activities are included.

Larrick, Nancy, and Merriam, Eve, eds. *Male & Female under 18.* New York: Avon, 1973. Selected from more than 2,500 replies to the question "How does it feel to be a girl or a boy today?" this anthology contains about 200 poems and brief prose statements by young people ages eight through eighteen. A useful topic index reveals the enormous variety of concerns beyond the expected ones, including games and sports, pride, school, work, jobs and discrimination.

LITERATURE/MULTI-MEDIA

To Be a Woman and a Writer. Guidance Associates. Dramatization of the prejudices and challenges women writers have encountered in the past four centuries. Part one concentrates on nineteenth-century authors, including Austen, Alcott and Brontë. Part two illustrates recurring themes of twentieth-century writers, including Olsen, Sexton, Hansberry, Woolf, Lessing. Includes two filmstrips plus guide, and records or cassettes.

INTERDISCIPLINARY

Abt Associates. *Career Education Activities for Subject Area Teachers.* Cambridge: Abt Associates, 1975. Developed for the National Institute of Education, these materials are consciously nonsexist in approach and language and represent an effort to infuse career education into existing subject areas. Volume II for grades six to nine and Volume III for grades nine to twelve—each an unbound looseleaf set of lesson sheets—contain activities for social studies, language arts, math, health, science, art and physical education.

Adams, Carol, and Laurikietis, Rae. *Book 1: Education and Work; Book 2: Sex and Marriage; Book 3: Messages and Images.* London: Virago-Limited, 1976. Available from Quartet Books. A series about the sex roles imposed on girls and boys in our society. *Book 1* looks at how children are raised, and how girls in particular have their options limited from an early age through schools, career expectations and work. *Book 2* examines the relationships between girls and boys and the role played by accepted ideas of masculinity and femininity. Sex and sex education are discussed together with contraception, abortion, medical issues, rape. *Book 3* deals with language and the media, showing how they reinforce and often create popular ideas about sex roles. A list of resources and bibliography is included in each book.

Ariosa, Gina et al. "Sex at an Early Age," *Women: A Journal of Liberation* 3 (1972):49-50. Four high school women talk about their socialization into sex roles and sexuality.

Brown, Nancy et al. *Abortion: Women's Fight for the Right to Choose.* New York: Pathfinder Press, 1975. This revised edition of a popular pamphlet takes up the struggle to extend and defend the Supreme Court victory American women won in January 1973. Included are such articles as "In Defense of the Right to Abortion," which explains why the supreme court decision was a victory for black women; "The Supreme Court Ruling on Abortion: How the Victory Was Won"; and "Abortion Rights under Attack," which describes the case of Dr. Kenneth Edelin, convicted of manslaughter for performing a legal abortion.

Cherniak, Donna, and Feingold, Allan. *Birth Control Handbook.* Montreal: The Handbook Collective, 1975. An excellent guide to information about birth control and abortion; the latest edition stresses men's as well as women's responsibility.

——. *V. D. Handbook.* Montreal: The Handbook Collective, 1975. This revised edition contains some of the best information for high school students about venereal disease.

Dispenza, Joseph E. *Advertising the American Woman.* Dayton: Pflaum Publishing, 1975. An anthology of advertising that points out how we have been conditioned to think about the roles of women in our society. Ads dating from 1900 to the present are organized around seven themes, among them: facial beauty, domestic relationships, romance and courtship, woman's shape, consumerism.

Feminists Northwest. *Planning for Free Lives.* Seattle: Feminists Northwest, 1975. These curricular materials for combating sex-stereotyping in home economics and family living classes include general awareness activities as well as suggestions for foods, sewing, family living and child development courses. "Whatever Happened to Debbie Kraft" is an awareness game in pamphlet form that poses the hypothetical (but realistic) situation of an 18-year-old about to graduate high school, who has to decide about college, work and marriage.

High School Women's Liberation. Ann Arbor: Youth Liberation Press, 1976. A collection of some 20 articles about liberation of interest to young women. Includes book reviews and poetry, as well as discussions of sexism in schools, textbooks, sports, lesbianism, black women and legal rights. One of the few materials written by and for high school women.

Merrick, Toni. *The American Woman: Her Image and Her Roles.* Columbus: Xerox Education Publications, 1975. Written especially for grades seven to twelve, this 64-page paperback on the status of women today contains sections that could be used as curriculum units to analyze male and female roles.

Project Equality. *Potpourri.* Seattle: The Highline School District, 1975. Various semester, nine-week and mini-course outlines which deal with career education, sex-role stereotyping, changing life styles, history and language.

Resource Center on Sex Roles in Education. *Today's Changing Roles: An Approach to Non-Sexist Teaching.* Washington: Resource Center on Sex Roles in Education, 1974. An excellent 108-page paperback designed as supplemental material to assist students explore and understand the limitations of sex-role stereotyping. For elementary, intermediate and secondary school teachers.

Status of Women Committee, San Fernando Branch, AAUW. *Jack and Jill.* 1972. Available from AAUW, California State Division. Written especially for high school students, this 30-page booklet contains exercises of sex-role stereotypes that are a model for developing school curriculum.

Somerville, Rose M. *Introduction to Family Life and Sex Education.* Englewood Cliffs: Prentice-Hall, 1972. A feminist textbook for students of family life and sex education.

Tax, Meredith. *Woman and Her Mind: The Story of Daily Life.* Somerville: New England Free Press, 1970. This provocative pamphlet describes and analyzes social and psychological forces that impinge on women—in the home, the family, at work and on the street.

Wells, Theodora. *Woman—Which Includes Man, of Course.* Beverly Hills: Wells Associates. A consciousness-raising essay for both students and teachers that includes useful exercises in sex-role stereotype analysis.

Women's Educational Project. *High School Sexuality: A Teaching Guide.* Eugene: Amazon Reality, n.d. A frank, enlightened sex-education pamphlet for high school women and men. Includes information on birth control, abortion, masturbation, homosexuality, sexual socialization, menstruation. Answers questions that high school students really ask.

INTERDISCIPLINARY/MULTI-MEDIA

The Cult of True Womanhood. Multimedia Productions. An excellent tool for dealing with male and female roles in the classroom. Two filmstrips, with record or cassette.

Herstory. Interact. A provocative simulation game for high school students emphasizing male and female roles in our society.

Male/Female: Changing Lifestyles. Educational Audio-Visual. These sound filmstrips focus on biological and behavioral differences with an emphasis on the history of sex roles.

Masculinity/Femininity. Guidance Associates. Two highly recommended filmstrips (with records or cassettes) from a company that has produced much useful material about sex roles.

The Role of Women in American Society.
Newton: EDC, 1976. A multi-unit program, each built around a half-hour documentary film of a stage in women's lives. Unit I, "Girls at 12" explores socialization: How did you learn to be a girl, or to be a boy? The Teacher's Guide provides a basis for classroom discussion, the Students Resource Book includes a bibliography and activities. Although the film is limited in that it looks at a small sector of society, the unit is valuable in any course that discusses the role of women. Unit II, "Clorae and Albie," features two young black women talking about how they are trying to create lives for themselves. The Resource Book makes a teaching package with the books that accompany the first unit.

Sex Stereotyping in the Schools. Available from Women's Education Resources. Slide tape series.

Woman and Man. Del Mar: C. R. M. Associates. A simulation game originally printed in *Psychology Today.*

A Woman's Place. Schloat Productions. A realistic, four-part examination of the current status of women in society: Images, Biology and Destiny, Myths, The Women's Movement. Program guides help turn the filmstrips into effective study units. Four color filmstrips, plus records or cassettes. As a companion filmstrip program, *Masculinity* examines man's position in a changing society.

Higher Education

RESOURCES FOR THE TEACHER This section lists readings and general resources in women's studies including guides to courses, volumes of syllabi and essays on teaching; and a number of major anthologies dealing with issues of employment and discrimination.

Abramson, Joan. *The Invisible Woman: Discrimination in the Academic Profession.* San Francisco: Jossey-Bass, 1975. This volume is in three parts. The first examines in some detail the case history of the author's own sex discrimination suit. Part two explores the academic setting and explains the establishment's control and how they maintain it. The last section describes the various methods of appeal women have open to them, the pitfalls and risks of legal action.

Babcock, Barbara et al. *Women and the Law: A Collection of Reading Lists.* Pittsburgh: KNOW, 1971.

Berkowitz, Tamar; Mangi, Jean; and Williamson, Jane, eds. *Who's Who and Where in Women's Studies.* Old Westbury: The Feminist Press, 1974. A directory of women's studies courses, teachers and programs in three lists: one by school, one by teacher and one by department.

Cassirer, Sidonie, ed. *Female Studies IX: Teaching about Women in the Foreign Languages.* Old Westbury: The Feminist Press, 1975. Includes articles and course outlines in French, Spanish and German studies.

Chmaj, Betty, ed. *American Women and American Studies.* Pittsburgh: KNOW, 1971. Includes a few course syllabi and essays, comparative analysis of several reports on the status of academic women and a personal, vivid account of the effect of the women's movement on academic women.

College English/Women in the Colleges: Status, Teaching, Feminist Criticism (May 1971). This special issue is an excellent source for the English teacher.

College English/Women Writing and Teaching (October 1972). This special issue is a collection of essays by women reflecting on their writing and teaching about women.

Hartnett, Oonagh, and Rendel, Margherita. *Women's Studies in the U. K.* London: The London Seminars, 1975. This 30-page booklet testifies to the internationality of the women's movement and women's studies. It lists women's studies courses, sources for teachers, a description of the London Seminars and questions for a future edition. Much like the first *Current Guide to Female Studies,* it is a valuable resource on women's studies in England.

Hoffman, Nancy; Secor, Cynthia; and Tinsley, Adrian, eds. *Female Studies VI: Closer to the Ground.* Old Westbury: The Feminist Press, 1972. Twenty-one essays on the practice of women's studies in the classroom, literary criticism from a feminist perspective, course materials.

Howe, Florence. *Female Studies II.* Pittsburgh: KNOW, 1970. Sixty-five course descriptions and bibliographies, plus five essays.

——, and Ahlum, Carol, eds. *Female Studies III.* Pittsburgh: KNOW, 1971. Fifty-four new course descriptions and bibliographies, descriptions of 17 wom-

43

en's studies programs and *Guide to Female Studies I.*

——. *Women and the Power to Change.* New York: McGraw-Hill, 1975. The effect of feminism as experienced by four academic women is charted in the histories of their lives in the world of higher education.

Kundsin, Ruth. *Women and Success: The Anatomy of Achievement.* New York: William Morrow, 1974. This anthology deals with the development of, attitudes toward and problems of professional women, particularly scientists. Family attitudes, the impact of education, economic factors and the women's individual life experiences are all explored.

McGuigan, Dorothy G. *New Research on Women and Sex Roles.* Ann Arbor: The University of Michigan, Center for Continuing Education, 1976. This anthology includes articles and abstracts reporting research on women and sex roles.

Project on the Status and Education of Women. *Women in the Curriculum.* Washington: Project on the Status of Education of Women, n.d. This paper is based on a comprehensive review of the literature on women's studies and provides an excellent introduction and overview. It describes the history of women's studies, defines its major objectives, analyzes the curricular and pedagogical issues. A basic, annotated bibliography is included.

Robinson, Lora H. *Women's Studies: Courses and Programs for Higher Education.* Washington: American Association for Higher Education, 1973. Pamphlet on women's studies courses and programs in the colleges.

Roby, Pamela. "Women and American Higher Education." *Annals of the American Academy of Political and Social Science* 404 (November 1972):118-139.

Rosenfelt, Deborah Silverton, ed. *Female Studies VII: Going Strong.* Old Westbury: The Feminist Press, 1973. Descriptions of 12 new programs and syllabi of 60 women's studies courses; introduction assesses recent developments and directions.

——. *Female Studies X: Student Work.* Old Westbury: The Feminist Press, 1975. Student papers in four categories: mothers and mothering, autobiography, research and creative work.

Rossi, Alice, and Calderwood, Ann, eds. *Academic Women on the Move.* New York: Russell Sage Foundation, 1973. This anthology is in three parts: recruitment, training and employment; women on the contemporary academic scene; action toward change. The research explains the history and social status of women in academe, documents the nature and range of sex discrimination and reports on the remedial efforts now being made.

Schramm, Sarah Slavin, ed. *Female Studies VIII: Do-It-Yourself Women's Studies.* Pittsburgh: KNOW, 1975.

Showalter, Elaine, and Ohmann, Carol, eds. *Female Studies IV.* Pittsburgh: KNOW, 1971. Includes an overview of feminist studies and 12 essays by teachers, as well as several bibliographical reports and reviews of current anthologies.

Siporin, Rae Lee, ed. *Female Studies V.* Pittsburgh: KNOW, 1971. Papers from a symposium on women's studies at the University of Pittsburgh.

"Teaching Women's Studies: A Teacher Paper Interview." *The Teacher Paper* 5 (December 1972):7-11.

Tobias, Sheila, ed. *Female Studies I.* Pittsburgh: KNOW, 1970. Seventeen course descriptions and bibliographies, chiefly in the social sciences.

Women's Equity Action League. *Higher Education Kit.* Washington: WEAL, 1976. The revised *Kit* includes items on federal laws and regulations concerning sex discrimination in educational institutions as well as information on filing complaints.

ANTHOLOGIES This compilation includes the major anthologies and texts on women in history, law, literature, anthropology and psychology. They were written for the college classroom, but many can also be used in advanced high school classes.

ANTHROPOLOGY

Reiter, Rayna R., ed. *Toward an Anthropology of Women.* New York; Monthly Review Press, 1975. The papers in this anthology provide some guidelines and examples of directions for a new anthropology of women. They include both theory and research.

Rosaldo, Michelle, and Lamphere, Louise, eds. *Woman, Culture and Society.* Stanford: Stanford University Press, 1974.

HISTORY

Carroll, Berenice, ed. *Liberating Women's History: Theoretical and Critical Essays.* Urbana: University of Illinois Press, 1976. An anthology of theoretical and critical essays in women's history collected with the intention of meeting the need for a critical historiography, to test old and new theories on a comparative basis, to find conceptual clarity and to help define new directions for research.

Cott, Nancy, ed. *Root of Bitterness.* New York: E. P. Dutton, 1972. Documents of the social history of American women from colonial times to 1900; selections from journals, autobiographies, fiction, manifestoes; source material for high school curriculum or background reading for the teacher.

Flexner, Eleanor, ed. *Century of Struggle.* New York: Atheneum, 1968. A classic on the history of American women from 1620 to the early twentieth century. Has recently been revised in hardcover (Harvard University Press, 1975).

James, Edward, and James, Janet, eds. *Notable American Women, 1607-1950.* Cambridge: The Belknap Press of Harvard University Press, 1974. This three-volume biographical dictionary of American women contains 1,379 carefully documented biographies spanning more than three centuries.

Kraditor, Aileen S., ed. *Up from the Pedestal: Selected Writings in American Feminism.* New York: Quadrangle, 1968. Primary source material useful as background reading for teachers and students and a source for high school curriculum.

Lerner, Gerda, ed. *The Black Woman in White America: A Documentary History.* New York: Vintage, 1973. First of its kind, this book collects major and unknown past and contemporary writings and oral history by and about black women; required reading for the history teacher.

Rossi, Alice S., ed. *The Feminist Papers: From Adams to de Beauvoir.* New York: Bantam, 1974. This 716-page volume chronicles the two hundred years of western feminist thought. It is impressive for its inclusiveness: 22 writers, plus selections from the *History of Woman Suffrage.*

Schneir, Miriam, ed. *Feminism: The Essential Historical Writings.* New York: Vintage, 1971. Documents by and about women throughout Western history both in Europe and the United States.

LAW

Babcock, Barbara et al. *Sex Discrimination and the Law: Causes and Remedies.* Boston: Little, Brown, 1975.

Ginsburg, Ruth Bader; Davidson, Kenneth; and Kay, Herma Hill. *Sex-Based Discrimination.* St. Paul: West Publishing, 1974.

Kanowitz, Leo. *Sex Roles in Law and Society: Cases and Materials.* Albuquerque: University of New Mexico Press, 1973.

LITERATURE

Cade, Toni, ed. *The Black Woman: An Anthology.* New York: New American Library, 1970. This collection contains contemporary writings by and about black women. It is one of the first anthologies presenting the black woman through her own eyes, in her own voice.

Cornillon, Susan Koppelman, ed. *Images of Women in Fiction: Feminist Perspectives.* Bowling Green: Bowling Green Popular Press, 1972. This wide-ranging collection of feminist literary criticism is a must for the English teacher; students will also enjoy many of the essays, which resolutely refuse to be pedantic.

Ellmann, Mary. *Thinking about Women.* New York: Harcourt, 1968. An investigation of literary conceptions of women from Jane Austen to Sylvia Plath, from D. H. Lawrence to Norman Mailer. A resource for the English teacher.

Ferguson, Mary Anne, ed. *Images of Women in Literature.* New York: Houghton-Mifflin, 1973. One of the best anthologies of its kind, this collection includes a wide and thoughtful selection of short stories, some poems and a short play. The selections are arranged according to stereotypes.

Goulianos, Joan, ed. *By a Woman Writt: Literature from Six Centuries by and about Women.* Baltimore: Penguin Books, 1973. This fine collection contains poems, short stories, essays and excerpts from longer works by women.

Moreno, Dorinda. *La Mujer—En Pie de Lucha.* Fremont, Cal.: Espina del Norte Publications, 1973. This singular folio of poems, essays, photographs, drawings, manifestoes, by and about Chicana women and other women of the Spanish-speaking Third World, reflects a consciousness both feminist and revolutionary. It demonstrates the diversity, strength and creativity of La Raza women.

Murray, Michele, ed. *A House of Good Proportion.* New York: Simon and Schuster, 1973. This anthology of poems, short stories and excerpts from novels is arranged chronologically according to the stages of a woman's life. The book is a useful basic text.

Parker, Gail, ed. *The Oven Birds.* New York: Anchor, 1972. Collection of little known works of fiction and journalism by American women on American womanhood from 1820-1920; source for high school curriculum.

Pearson, Carol, and Pope, Katherine, eds. *Who Am I This Time? Female Portraits in British and American Literature.* New York: McGraw-Hill, 1976. This anthology of poetry and short stories is divided into two major parts: the Heroine and the Hero. The selections in the Heroine include portraits of women which are predominantly stereotypical or archetypal; the Hero section traces an alternative tradition of female characterization.

Showalter, Elaine, ed. *Women's Liberation*

and Literature. New York: Harcourt, 1971. This anthology contains substantial excerpts from Mary Wollstonecraft and John Stuart Mill, all of Ibsen's *A Doll House,* a few poems and short stories and helpful selections in literary criticism (including Virginia Woolf and Kate Millett) and women and psychology (including Betty Friedan).

PSYCHOLOGY

Cox, Sue, ed. *Female Psychology: The Emerging Self.* Chicago: Science Research Associates, 1976. This textbook of feminist psychology is excellent. It includes many classic articles in eight sections. The introductory sections take a frankly feminist stand and set the articles in a larger context.

Sources of Further Information

BIBLIOGRAPHY This compilation is not meant to be exhaustive. It includes, rather, several of the major general bibliographies on women and several of those on women's education, including other curriculum guides like this one. Specific subject-oriented bibliographies appear in the appropriate sections throughout.

GENERAL BIBLIOGRAPHIES

Bruemmer, Linda. "The Condition of Women in Society Today: A Review." *National Association of Women Deans and Counselors* 33 (Fall 1969):18-22 and 33 (Winter 1970):89-95. A review of the literature from 1966 on the various patterns of life and options in lifestyle for women today.

Cardinale, Susan. *Special Issues of Serials about Women, 1965-1975.* Monticello, Ill.: Council of Planning Librarians, 1976. This bibliography provides a much-needed handle on the myriad special issues on women. The citations are alphabetical by journal title and are selectively annotated. This list is very comprehensive and covers a wide subject range.

Cisler, Lucinda. *Women: A Bibliography.* 1970. Available from Lucinda Cisler. This partially annotated bibliography is one of the first women's bibliographies to appear and has been the personal project of Ms. Cisler through six editions. It is classified into 14 subjects and also includes a periodical list. Notations indicate editions in paperback and those worthy of special attention. It has much historical material and much that is new.

Cole, Johnetta. "Black Women in America: An Annotated Bibliography." *Black Scholar* 3 (December 1971):42-53.

Daniels, Arlene Kaplan. *A Survey of Research Concerns on Women's Issues.* Washington: Project on the Status and Education of Women, 1975. This pamphlet is a comprehensive review of the literature in the central areas of research relating to women.

ERIC. The Educational Resources Information Center (ERIC) is a nation-wide network of 16 clearinghouses. Each clearinghouse acquires educational material in its subject field. Among these materials are curriculum guides, teaching units, games, descriptions of innovative programs, bibliographies and research reports. Once acquired, they are summarized and indexed in the monthly publication, *Resource in Education,* and are made available in microfiche and/or hard copy. ERIC is particularly valuable since it provides access to "fugitive" materials—those that are not commercially published and easily available. Unfortunately, its massiveness and computer base scare off many potential users. The 16 topics covered by the clearinghouses are: career education; counseling and personnel services; early childhood education; educational management; handicapped and gifted children; higher education; information resources; junior colleges; languages and linguistics; reading and communication skills; rural education and small schools; science, mathematics and environmental education; teacher education; tests, measurement and evaluation; urban education; and social studies/social science education. While there is no center for women's studies, all the banks contain information relevant to women in the curriculum and other issues. A complete computer search can be done to locate all materials on a particular subject, such as women. A search costs $16.50 for up to 50 citations and 10¢ per citation after that. ERIC is a useful tool for teachers, parents, librarians and administrators.

Friedman, Barbara et al. *Women's Work and Women's Studies, 1973-74.* New York: The Women's Center, Barnard College, 1975. Available from The Feminist Press. Annual interdisciplinary bibliography covering the year's scholarship in women's studies, including work in progress. Partially annotated, subject classification, author index. Compilations for 1971 and 1972 are available from KNOW, Inc.

Grimstad, Kirsten, and Rennie, Susan. *The New Woman's Survival Sourcebook.* New York: Alfred A. Knopf, 1975. A *complete* guide to the current women's movement in all its aspects across the country. Includes presses, publications, film projects, theatre, day care, health, books, schools, rape, employment and an extensive list of women's groups. Heavily and well illustrated.

Harrison, Cynthia Ellen. *Women's Movement Media: A Source Guide.* New York: R. R. Bowker, 1975. This is not a bibliography, but a guide to sources of information. It includes approximately 550 descriptions of organizations, arranged by function, type or main interest of group, and what materials they supply. There are geographic, title, group name and subject indexes.

Rosenberg, Marie B., and Bergstrom, Len V. *Women and Society: A Critical Review of the Literature with a Selected Annotated Bibliography.* New York: Sage Publications, 1975. Includes approximately 3600 entries primarily in the social sciences and humanities. Criteria for selection were that the work be generally authoritative and available and constitute "scholarly and applied research efforts."

Wheeler, Helen. *Womanhood Media Supplement (to Womanhood Media: Current Resources, 1972).* Metuchen: Scarecrow Press, 1975. The Supplement to Helen Wheeler's original compilation reprints the bulk of the material, and therefore, supercedes it. The Basic Book Collection lists fiction by author and nonfiction by subject; Non-book Resources are listed by type of resource. It is very comprehensive and useful.

Williams, Ora. *American Black Women in the Arts and Social Sciences: A Bibliographic Survey.* Metuchen: Scarecrow Press, 1973. The bibliography contains over 1200 entries of works by American black women including print and nonprint media. There is a comprehensive listing subdivided by subject, a section on black women in the graphic arts and music, listings of audio-visual aids, periodicals and black publishing houses. There is a name index and there are selected portraits throughout.

Women's Studies Abstracts, P. O. Box 1, Rush, NY 14543. This quarterly journal includes a book review essay, book reviews and abstracts which are arranged by subject. Articles for which there are no abstractions are given just a listing. Author, subject indexes.

EDUCATION BIBLIOGRAPHIES

Astin, Helen S.; Suniewick, Nancy; and Dweck, Susan. *Women: A Bibliography on Their Education and Careers.* Washington: Human Service Press, 1971. This bibliography covers research materials from the last decade for the most part, though some items from the 1950's are included. The citations are arranged by subject into seven chapters and one for miscellaneous. Entries are annotated and there are author and subject indexes.

Barabos, Jean. *Women: Their Education and Career Goals: An Annotated Bibliography of Selected ERIC References.* ERIC, 1972. (ED 067 423).

Elkin, Anna. *The Emerging Role of Mature Women: Basic Background Data in Employment and Continuing Education.* New York: Federation Employment and Guidance Service, 1976.

Haller, Elizabeth S. *Images of Women: A Bibliography of Feminist Resources for Pennsylvania Schools.* Harrisburg: Department of Education, 1973. This resource booklet was compiled to help Pennsylvania schools comply with Memorandum 544 calling for an end to sexist practices in the public schools. It includes annotated sections on biography, careers, fiction, history, the arts and the women's movement. There is a section on stereotypes in trade and textbooks, a brief guide to nonprint media and a list of other resources.

Harmon, Linda A. *Status of Women in Higher Education: 1963-1972, A Selective Bibliography.* Ames, Iowa: Iowa State University, 1972. The bibliography covers only U. S. material and the citations are arranged into chapters according to type of material—books, articles, government publications, dissertations, ERIC and ephemera. There is no index.

Hart, Lois B. *A Feminist Looks at Educational Software.* Amherst: Everywoman's Center, University of Massachusetts.

Leib, Prudence. *Sex Roles: Past, Present and Future.* Washington: The Population Institute, 1975. This annotated list is in two parts: games on feminism and sexism and vocational simulation games. The annotations provide suggestions for use and age/grade level.

Olin, Ferris. *Fair Play: A Bibliography of Nonstereotyped Materials.* New Brunswick: Training Institute for Sex Desegregation of the Public Schools, Douglass College, 1976. The materials are organized by both subject and grade level. An excellent resource.

Software Committee, Sexism in Education Conference. *Recommended Nonstereotyped Software and Educational Materials.* 1975. Available from Arlene Metha. This annotated list includes a wide variety of materials of use to the teacher including records, tapes, films, filmstrips, posters and photographs. Grade level is indicated.

Westervelt, Esther, and Fixter, Deborah. *Women's Higher and Continuing Education, An Annotated Bibliography.* New York: College Entrance Examination Board, 1971. The primary focus of this list is women's higher and continuing education with secondary emphasis on women's employment. It is a highly select list that tries to cover and represent a broad spectrum of materials; items were chosen for quality, representativeness and timeliness. No foreign language materials are included and there is no index.

GUIDES TO NONPRINT RESOURCES Films by or about women have proliferated in the last few years. Because of this recent activity, there are now excellent guides to these films in print. This section lists several of the best of these guides and also a number of producers of audio tapes about women.

Audio Visual Center. *Women's Films—A Critical Guide*. Bloomington: Indiana University, 1975. This *Guide* is the result of several months of film viewing and evaluating. It lists the films by subject and includes a title index, distributor list with addresses, a bibliography for further searching and list of late releases.

Betancourt, Jeanne. *Women in Focus.* Dayton: Pflaum Publishing, 1974. This is probably the best film guide for the teacher. It annotates over 75 films by and about women, categorizes them by subject and provides ideas for use in the classroom as well as readings to accompany each film. It includes distributors, their addresses and price information.

Film Library Quarterly/Women in Film (Winter 1971-72). This special issue is one of the best collections of information about women in film; contains analysis and reviews.

Liberation Media, Women Involvement Program, 341 Bloor St. W, #309, Toronto, Ontario, Canada. Write for list of available audio tapes.

Pacifica Tape Library, 5316 Venice Blvd., Los Angeles, CA 90019. Write for catalog of audio tapes on women listing over 150 programs.

Sounds from Within, 26 W. 20 St., New York, NY 10011. Write for catalog of available audio tapes.

Wengraf, Susan. *Positive Images: A Guide to Nonsexist Films for Young People.* San Francisco: Booklegger Press, 1976.

Women and Film, P. O. Box 4501. Berkeley, CA 94704. Published tri-annually.

Women's History Research Center. *Films by and/or about Women.* Berkeley: Women's History Research Center, 1972. An extensive directory of women filmmakers, films and distributors.

ORGANIZATIONS This section lists a number of organizations working for the elimination of sex discrimination in the schools at all levels. Their activities are wide-ranging and include research, lobbying, publishing, teaching.

American Association of University Women, 2401 Virginia Ave. N.W., Washington, D C 20037. Write to the Association for the latest listing of women's caucuses, committees and professional associations.

American Federation of Teachers, Women's Rights Committee, 1012 14 St., N.W., Washington, D C 20005. This group has produced a number of pamphlets about rights for the woman teacher; write for a listing.

Change for Children, 2588 Mission St., #226, San Francisco, CA 94110. This multi-ethnic resource center and library is concerned with nonsexist education. It assists child-care centers, pre- and elementary schools, and has produced a number of excellent materials.

Cornelia Wheadon Task Force, Women's Liberation Center, 2214 Ridge Ave., Evanston, IL 60201. Task Force members include parents and teachers who are concerned about the detrimental effects of sex-role stereotyping on children. Their objectives include providing information and resources, putting pressure on publishers and schools and raising the consciousness of teachers.

Emma Willard Task Force on Education, P. O. Box 14229, University Station, Minneapolis, MN 55414. The Task Force is a group of feminists working to combat sexism in the schools. They are an excellent resource for Minnesota teachers; their materials are available nationally.

Feminists Northwest, 5038 Nicklas Pl. N.E., Seattle, WA 98105. This nonprofit education group has worked to combat sexism in the schools in a number of ways. They have: developed nonsexist curriculum, produced a slide show on stereotyping in elementary textbooks, worked with teachers.

National Education Association, Customer Service Section, 1201 16 St. N.W., Washington, D C 20036. Write for their brochure of nonsexist print and audio-visual materials.

National Organization for Women, 5 S. Wabash, #1615, Chicago, IL 60603. One of the national organizations that has grown out of the current feminist movement, NOW has many local chapters and local Education Task Forces. Write for addresses.

Ontario Institute for Studies in Education, 252 Bloor St. W., Toronto, Ontario, Canada M5S 1V6. *The Women's Kit* (records, slides, articles, posters, photos, plays, poems, stories) began as a curriculum project and is now an entire department. Write for more information.

Project on Equal Education Rights, 1029 Vermont Ave. N.W., Washington, D C 20005. This Project of the NOW Legal Defense and Education Fund monitors and disseminates information on the enforcement of Title IX in elementary and secondary schools. Write to receive their newsletter.

Project on the Status and Education of Women, Association of American Colleges, 1818 R St. N.W., Washington D C 20009. The Project compiles materials on women in higher education, including legal developments, federal action on employment, women's groups on campus, women's studies. Founded in 1971. Write to receive their newsletter.

Racism and Sexism Resource Center for Educators (Council on Interracial Books for Children), 1841 Broadway, #300, New York, NY 10023. The Council opened in 1965 as a voluntary group of concerned editors, librarians and writers to initiate needed change in the all-white world of children's books. Since then, it has grown enormously and produced a wide variety of materials. The Resource Center develops original materials, provides training and conducts workshops for schools and other groups, evaluates text and trade books and maintains a resource library. Write for their catalog.

Resource Center on Sex Roles in Education, 1201 16 St. N.W., Washington, D C 20036. The Center's three primary functions are to develop materials for use by administrators, teachers, parents and students; to operate a clearinghouse of resource persons and materials; to provide technical assistance to states and other groups in developing or implementing programs for equal opportunity in education. Write for a list of publications.

Research Center on Women, Alverno College, 3401 S. 39 St., Milwaukee, WI 53215. A center for its own college, but also for other organizations and individuals. Contains a growing library of feminist periodicals, books, audio and visual tapes and an information file on women's lives. A good resource for Midwest teachers.

Women's Equity Action League, 821 National Press Bldg., Washington, D C 20004. A nonprofit, tax-exempt organization which helps to pay costs of legal cases, sponsors research and publishes material on sex discrimination. Its priorities are women in the military, women and sports, women and work and education.

Women on Words and Images, P. O. Box 2163, Princeton, NJ 08540. One of the earliest groups to analyze textbooks, they produced *Dick and Jane as Victims* in 1972. Since then they have done work on sexism in career education materials and foreign language textbooks.

Women's Action Alliance, 370 Lexington Ave., New York, NY 10017. A non-profit, educational organization established in 1971 to help translate a growing awareness of sex discrimination into concrete actions, it offers information, research resources, model projects, referral. A major project on sex-role stereotyping in early childhood includes inservice teacher training, parent education and materials development.

Women's Bureau, U. S. Department of Labor, Washington, D C 20210. Write for their publications list of over 75 excellent resources. Much of the material is free and most of it is of use in the classroom.

PERIODICALS This list includes newsletters and journals of two kinds: those from the women's movement and those concerned with women and education. The compilation is certainly not exhaustive, but represents a selection that is both wide-ranging and useful for the classroom. The address listed is for subscription information.

Aphra, P. O. Box 893, Ansonia Station, New York, NY 10023. Quarterly feminist literary journal of prose and poetry; a good source of material by and about women for English classes.

E.E.O. Reporter, P. O. Box 391, Madison, NJ 07940. Bi-monthly newsletter on equal educational opportunity, provides accurate and authoritative information on employee rights, litigation and court cases.

ERIC/Early Childhood Education Newsletter, University of Illinois, 805 W. Pennsylvania Ave., Urbana, IL 61801.

The Feminist Art Journal, 41 Montgomery Pl., Brooklyn, NY 11215. Quarterly about women's art and art history, primarily the visual arts, but includes poetry, film, drama.

Feminist Studies, 417 Riverside Dr., New York, NY 10025. Quarterly journal of analytic responses to current feminist issues; concentrates primarily in history.

Media Report to Women, 3306 Ross Pl. N.W., Washington, D C 20008. Monthly report on "what women are doing and thinking about the communications media"–facts, actions, ideas and philosophy.

Ms., 123 Garden, Marion, OH 43302. This monthly is a useful periodical for teachers and students of women's studies; includes articles about forgotten women in history, samples of nonsexist children's stories, information about skills that women have rarely learned and articles about and by men. Useful as supplementary classroom material.

Research Action Notes, Resource Center on Sex Roles in Education, 1201 16 St. N.W., Washington, D C 20036. This newsletter reports on recent research in sex roles and education, new developments in the law, etc.

Second Wave, P. O. Box 344, Cambridge A, Cambridge, MA 02139. Monthly journal of feminist issues, reporting Boston and national news and analysis.

Sex Discrimination in Education Newsletter, Department of Psychology, University of Michigan, Ann Arbor, MI 48104. A new publication to facilitate communication and share resources in combating sex discrimination in education.

Signs: A Journal of Women in Culture and Society, University of Chicago Press, 11030 Langley Ave., Chicago, IL 60628. Quarterly journal that is both international and interdisciplinary.

The Spokeswoman, 5464 South Shore Dr., Chicago, IL 60615. This independent monthly newsletter for women includes analysis of the critical issues with coverage of the news.

Women: A Journal of Liberation, 3028 Greenmount Ave., Baltimore, MD 21218. Quarterly of feminist issues; excellent resource for teachers and students of women's studies. Useful as supplementary material in classrooms.

Women Today, National Press Bldg., Washington, D C 20004. This bi-weekly newsletter keeps track of women in the news, as well as issues and current events of importance to women.

Women's Rights Law Reporter, 180 University Ave., Newark, NJ 07102. Quarterly report of legal developments affecting women; includes articles on important cases.

Women's Studies, Gordon and Breach Science Publishers, One Park Ave., New York, NY 10016. Quarterly interdisciplinary journal about the study of women; a resource for the teacher of women's studies.

Women's Studies Newsletter, The Feminist Press, P. O. Box 334, Old Westbury, NY 11568. Quarterly of information on and analysis of feminist curriculum, with articles from teachers of women's studies; includes pieces on elementary and secondary teaching.

Women's Work, Washington Opportunities for Women, 1111 20 St. N.W., Washington, D C 20036. Bi-monthly magazine providing information about employment for women: job ideas, employment trends, listings, resources, etc.

PUBLISHERS/BOOK DISTRIBUTORS   This section reflects the growth of alternative publishing organizations across the country. It lists many of the major women's publishers of both adult and children's books and the distributors of alternate materials.

DISTRIBUTORS

Child's Play, 226 Atlantic Ave., Brooklyn, NY 11201. Write for their catalog of books, toys.

Feminist Book Mart, 47-17 150 St., Flushing, NY 11355. Write for catalog of nonsexist materials for people from three years to adult.

First Things First, P. O. Box 9041, Washington, D C 20003. Write for catalog of nonsexist books for women and children.

Learn Me, 642 Grand Ave., St. Paul, MN 55105. Write for catalog of over 700 items including children's books, puzzles, games, toys—all selected with an eye to avoiding stereotyped images of people by sex, race, class and national origin.

Women in Distribution, P. O. Box 8858, Washington, D C 20003. Write for catalog of over 160 titles by women's publishing concerns.

PRESSES

Alice James Books, 138 Mt. Auburn St., Cambridge, MA 02138. Publishes poetry only.

Before We Are Six, 15 King St. N., Waterloo, Ontario, Canada. Nonsexist children's books.

Belladonna Publishing, 844 Elm St., New Haven, CT 06511. Adult nonfiction.

Canadian Women's Educational Press, 305-280 Bloor St. W., Toronto, Ontario, Canada. Nonsexist children's and adults' books.

Daughters, Inc., Plainfield, VT 05667. Adult fiction.

Diana Press, 12 W. 25 St., Baltimore, MD 21218. Publisher and printer.

The Feminist Press, P. O. Box 334, Old Westbury, NY 11568. Nonsexist children's books, reprints of literature by women, biographies and nonsexist educational materials.

Greyfalcon House, 60 Riverside Dr., New York, NY 10024. Nonsexist children's books, posters, stationery, adult books.

Joyful World Press, 468 Belvedere St., San Francisco, CA 94117. Nonsexist children's books.

Kids Can Press, P. O. Box 5974, Postal Station A, Toronto, Ontario, Canada. Nonsexist children's books.

KNOW, P. O. Box 86031, Pittsburgh, PA 15221. Extensive selection of articles, reprints and materials for women's studies courses.

Lollipop Power, P. O. Box 1171, Chapel Hill, NC 27514. Nonsexist children's books.

New England Free Press, 60 Union Sq., Somerville, MA 02143. Extensive selection of articles and pamphlets, many about women.

New Seed Press, P. O. Box 3016, Stanford, CA 94305. Nonsexist children's books.

The Shameless Hussy Press, P. O. Box 424, San Lorenzo, CA 94580. Publishes fiction and poetry.

Times Change Press, P. O. Box 98, Louisa, VA 23093. Extensive selection of books, pamphlets, posters about current issues. They have a special catalog of cloth editions for libraries.

United Sisters, 4312 West Bay Ave., Tampa, FL 33616. Publishes fiction and poetry.

The Women's Press Collective, 5251 Broadway, Oakland, CA 94610. Publishes poetry.

List of Publishers

AAUW California State Division
  Box 661
  Livermore, CA 94550
Abt Associates, Inc.
  55 Wheeler St.
  Cambridge, MA 02138
Academy Press, Ltd.
  176 Williams St.
  Chicago, IL 60603
Addison-Wesley Publishing Co.
  Reading, MA 01867
Ad-hoc Committee for Women
  and Girls in Education
  3409 S.W. Trenton St.
  Seattle, WA 98126
Alpha Kappa Alpha Sorority, Inc.
  5211 S. Greenwood Ave.
  Chicago, IL 60615
Amazon Reality
  P. O. Box 95
  Eugene, OR 97401
American Association for Higher Education
  1 Dupont Circle, #780
  Washington, DC 20036
American Association of Health, Physical
  Education and Recreation
  1201 16 St. N.W.
  Washington, DC 20036
American Association of School Administrators
  1801 N. Moore St.
  Arlington, VA 22209
American Civil Liberties Union
  22 E. 40 St.
  New York, NY 10016
American College Testing Program
  P. O. Box 168
  Iowa City, IA 52240
American Education Week
  P. O. Box 327
  Hyattsville, MD 20781
American Federation of Teachers
  Women's Rights Committee
  1012 14 St. N.W.
  Washington, DC 20005
American Personnel and Guidance Association
  1607 New Hampshire Ave. N.W.
  Washington, DC 20009
Anchor Press/Doubleday
  245 Park Ave.
  New York, NY 10017
Atheneum
  122 E. 42 St.
  New York, NY 10017
Avon Books

Customer Service
  250 W. 55 St.
  New York, NY 10019

Balick, Nancy L.
  1801 E. 12 St.
  Cleveland, OH 44114
Bantam Books
  666 Fifth Ave.
  New York, NY 10019
BARTOC
  388 Sanchez
  San Francisco, CA 94114
Basic Books
  10 E. 53 St.
  New York, NY 10022
Behavioral Publications, Inc.
  72 Fifth Ave.
  New York, NY 10011
The Belknap Press of Harvard University Press
  79 Garden St.
  Cambridge, MA 02138
Benziger
  8701 Wilshire Blvd.
  Beverly Hills, CA 90211
Berkeley Unified School District
  1414 Walnut St.
  Berkeley, CA 94709
B'nai B'rith
  Career and Counseling Services
  1640 Rhode Island Ave. N.W.
  Washington, DC 20036
Booklegger Press
  555 29 St.
  San Francisco, CA 94131
Boston Area Women in Libraries
  c/o Cyrisse Jaffe
  108 Pearson Rd.
  Somerville, MA 02144
R. R. Bowker Co.
  1180 Sixth Ave.
  New York, NY 10036
Bowling Green Popular Press
  Bowling Green University
  Bowling Green, OH 43402
Business and Professional Women's Foundation
  2012 Massachusetts Ave. N.W.
  Washington, DC 20036

Cade, Cathy
  2103 Emerson St.
  Berkeley, CA 94705

Caedmon Records
505 Eighth Ave.
New York, NY 10018
California Council for the Social Studies
2205 Sixteenth St.
Sacramento, CA 95818
Cambridge Book Co.
488 Madison Ave.
New York, NY 10022
Canadian Women's Educational Press
280 Bloor St. W., #305
Toronto, Ont.
Canada
Career Futures, Inc.
2100 Locust St.
Philadelphia, PA 19103
Career Women in Education
65 Central Park Rd.
Plainview, NY 11803
Center for New Directions
Los Angeles Valley College
5800 Fulton Ave.
Van Nuys, CA 91401
The Center for Vocational Education
The Ohio State University
1960 Kenny Rd.
Columbus, OH 43210
Change for Children
2588 Mission St., #226
San Francisco, CA 94110
Charles A. Jones Publishing Co.
4 Village Green S.E.
Worthington, OH 43805
Childcraft Education Corp.
20 Kilmer Rd.
Edison, NJ 08817
Choice for Tomorrow
P. O. Box 1455
Cupertino, CA 95014
Cisler, Lucinda
P. O. Box 240
Planetarium Station
New York, NY 10024
College Entrance Examination Board
P. O. Box 2815
Princeton, NJ 98540
The Conference Board, Inc.
845 Third Ave.
New York, NY 10022
Connecticut Public Interest Research Group
P. O. Box 1571
Hartford, CT 01601
Contemporary Press
P. O. Box 24338
San Jose, CA 95194
David C. Cook
850 N. Grove Ave.
Elgin, IL 60120

Council of Planning Librarians
P. O. Box 229
Monticello, IL 61856
C.R.M. Associates
1331 Camino Del Mar
Del Mar, CA 92014
Thomas Y. Crowell Co.
666 Fifth Ave.
New York, NY 10019

David C. Cook
850 N. Grove Ave.
Elgin, IL 60120
Davis, Enid
1050 Newell Rd.
Palo Alto, CA 94303
Dayton Public Schools
c/o Joyce Kaser
348 West First St.
Dayton, OH 45402
Dell Publishing Co.
245 E. 47 St.
New York, NY 10017
Documentary Photo Aids
P. O. Box 2620
Sarasota, FL 33578
Dun-Donnelly Publishing Corp.
Systems and Seminars Division
666 Fifth Ave.
New York, NY 10019
E. P. Dutton and Co.
201 Park Ave. S.
New York, NY 10003

EDC
39 Chapel St.
Newton, MA 02160
Education Commission of the States
300 Lincoln Tower
1860 Lincoln St.
Denver, CO 80203
Educational Activities, Inc.
P. O. Box 392
Freeport, NY 11520
Educational Audio-Visual, Inc.
17 Marble Ave.
Pleasantville, NY 10570
ERIC Clearinghouses:
Career Education
204 Gabel Hall
Northern Illinois University
DeKalb, IL 60115
Counseling and Personnel Services
University of Michigan
School of Education Bldg., #2180
Ann Arbor, MI 48109
Early Childhood Education

University of Illinois
College of Education
805 W. Pennsylvania Ave.
Urbana, IL 61801
Educational Management
University of Oregon
Eugene, OR 97403
Handicapped and Gifted Children
The Council for Exceptional Children
1920 Association Dr.
Reston, VA 22091
Higher Education
George Washington University
1 Dupont Circle N.W., #630
Washington, DC 20036
Information Resources
Center for Research and Development
in Teaching
Stanford University
School of Education
Stanford, CA 94305
Junior Colleges
University of California
Powell Library, #96
Los Angeles, CA 90024
Languages and Linguistics
Center for Applied Linguistics
1611 N. Kent St.
Arlington, VA 22209
Reading and Communication Skills
National Council of Teachers of English
1111 Kenyon Rd.
Urbana, IL 61801
Rural Education and Small Schools
New Mexico State University
Box 3 AP
Las Cruces, NM 88003
Science, Mathematics and Environmental
Education
Ohio State University
1200 Chambers Rd., 3 Fl.
Columbus, OH 43212
Teacher Education
American Association of Colleges for
Teacher Education
1 Dupont Circle N.W., #616
Washington, DC 20036
Tests, Measurements and Evaluation
Educational Testing Service
Princeton, NJ 08540
Urban Education
Teachers College
Columbia University
525 W. 120 St.
Box 40
New York, NY 10027
Emma Willard Task Force on Education
P. O. Box 14229

University Station
Minneapolis, MN 55414
Encyclopaedia Britannica
Educational Corp.
3712 Jarvis Ave.
Skokie, IL 60076
Ernest, John
Mathematics Department
University of California
Santa Barbara, CA 93106
Espina del Norte Publications
4885 Los Arboles
Fremont, CA 94536
Everywoman Center
University of Massachusetts
Amherst, MA 01002

Far West Laboratory
1855 Folsom St.
San Francisco, CA 94103
Fawcett World Library
1515 Broadway
New York, NY 10036
Federation Employment and Guidance Service
215 Park Ave. S.
New York, NY 10003
Feminist Book Mart
47-15 150 St.
Flushing, NY 11355
Feminist History Research Project
P. O. Box 1156
Topanga, CA 90290
The Feminist Press
P. O. Box 334
Old Westbury, NY 11568
Feminist Resources for Equal Education
P. O. Box 3185
Saxonville Station
Framingham, MA 01701
Feminists Northwest
5038 Nicklas Pl. N.E.
Seattle, WA 98105
Folkway Records
701 Seventh Ave.
New York, NY 10036
Fort Worth Educational Task Force, NOW
930 S. Fifth St.
Fort Worth, TX 76019
Franklin Watts
730 Fifth Ave.
New York, NY 10019
Free to Be Foundation
370 Lexington Ave.
New York, NY 10017
Fundamentals
P. O. Box 263
South Pasadena, CA 91030

Garrard Publishing Co.
1607 N. Market St.
Champaign, IL 61820
Glencoe Press
8701 Wilshire Blvd.
Beverly Hills, CA 90211
Government Printing Office
Superintendent of Documents
Washington, DC 20402
Green, Cynthia P.
1718 P St. N.W., #619
Washington, DC 20036
Grossman Publishers/Viking Press
625 Madison Ave.
New York, NY 10022
Guidance Associates
Distribution Center
Castleton St.
Pleasantville, NY 10570

The Handbook Collective
P. O. Box 1000, Station G
Montreal, Que. H2W2N1
Canada
Harcourt Brace Jovanovich
757 Third Ave.
New York, NY 10017
Harper and Row
10 E. 53 St.
New York, NY 10022
Highline Public School District 401
P. O. Box 66100
Seattle, WA 98166
Hogtown Press
12 Hart House Circle
University of Toronto
Toronto, Ont.
Canada
Holt, Rhinehart and Winston
383 Madison Ave.
New York, NY 10017
Houghton-Mifflin Co.
1 Beacon St.
Boston, MA 02107
Human Interaction Research Institute
10889 Wilshire Blvd.
Los Angeles, CA 90024
Human Sciences Press
72 Fifth Ave.
New York, NY 10011

University of Illinois Press
Urbana, IL 61801
Indiana University
Audio Visual Center
Bloomington, IN 47401

Institute for Educational Leadership
George Washington University
1001 Connecticut Ave. N.W.
Washington, DC 20036
Instructo Corp.
Paoli, PA 19301
Interact
P. O. Box 262
Lakeside, CA 92040
Iowa State University
Ames, IA 50010

Jerome S. Ozer
475 Fifth Ave.
New York, NY 10017
Charles A. Jones Publishing Co.
4 Village Green S.E.
Worthington, OH 43805
Jossey-Bass Publishers
615 Montgomery St.
San Francisco, CA 94111
Judy Puzzles
General Learning Corp.
Minneapolis, MN 55401
Julian Messner/Simon and Schuster
1 W. 39 St.
New York, NY 10018

Kalamazoo Public Schools
Instructional Media Dept.
1220 Howard St.
Kalamazoo, MI 49008
Kendall/Hunt Publishing Co.
2460 Kerper Blvd.
Dubuque, IA 52001
Alfred A. Knopf, Inc.
201 E. 50 St.
New York, NY 10022
KNOW, Inc.
P. O. Box 86031
Pittsburgh, PA 15221

Lexington School Committee
1557 Massachusetts Ave.
Lexington, MA 02173
Little, Brown and Co.
34 Beacon St.
Boston, MA 02106
Liveright/W. W. Norton
500 Fifth Ave.
New York, NY 10036
The London Seminars
c/o M. Rendel
71 Clifton Rd.
London NW8 OJN England

Lothrop, Lee and Shepard Co.
105 Madison Ave.
New York, NY 10016

Macmillan Publishing Co.
866 Third, Ave.
New York, NY 10022
Maferr Foundation
124 E. 28 St.
New York, NY 10016
Massachusetts Department of Education
Bureau of Equal Educational Opportunity
182 Tremont St.
Boston, MA 02111
McGraw-Hill Book Co.
1221 Avenue of the Americas
New York, NY 10020
Media Plus
60 Riverside Dr., #11D
New York, NY 10024
Menard, Sharon L.
2348 N. 107 St.
Lafayette, CO 80026
Julian Messner/Simon and Schuster
1 W. 39 St.
New York, NY 10018
Metha, Arlene
Software Committee for the Conference
on Sexism in Education
Arizona State University
Tempe, AZ 85821
Michigan State University
Counseling Center
207 Student Services Bldg.
East Lansing, MI 48824
University of Michigan
Center for Continuing Education of Women
Ann Arbor, MI 48104
Michigan Women's Commission
230 N. Washington
Lansing, MI 48933
Minnesota Department of Education
Capitol Square
500 Cedar St.
St. Paul, MN 55101
M.I.T. Press
77 Massachusetts Ave.
Cambridge, MA 02139
Monthly Review Press
62 W. 14 St.
New York, NY 10011
William Morrow and Co.
105 Madison Ave.
New York, NY 10016
Multimedia Productions
P. O. Box 5097
Stanford, CA 94305

National Assessment of Educational
Progress
700 Lincoln Tower
Denver, CO 80203
National Council for the Social Studies
1515 Wilson Blvd.
Arlington, VA 22209
National Council of Teachers of English
1111 Kenyon Rd.
Urbana, IL 61801
National Education Association
Customer Service Section
1201 16 St. N.W.
Washington, DC 20036
National Institute of Education
1200 19 St. N.W.
Washington, DC 20208
National Organization of Women (NOW)
5 S. Wabash, #1615
Chicago, IL 60603
(Write for address of local chapter)
National Project on Ethnic America
American Jewish Committee
165 E. 65 St.
New York, NY 10022
New American Library
1301 Sixth Ave.
New York, NY 10019
New England Free Press
60 Union Sq.
Somerville, MA 02143
University of New Mexico Press
Albuquerque, NM 87131
New York State Education Dept.
State University of New York
Division of Curriculum Development
Albany, NY 12234
News and Letters Committees
1900 E. Jefferson
Detroit, MI 48207
Nickerson, Eileen T.
Boston University
111 Cummington St., #240
Boston, MA 02215

Office of Equal Educational Opportunity
Michigan Department of Education
P. O. Box 420
Lansing, MI 48902
The Ontario Institute for Studies
in Education
252 Bloor St. W.
Toronto, Ont.
Canada
Jerome S. Ozer
475 Fifth Ave.
New York, NY 10017

Pantheon Books
201 E. 50 St.
New York, NY 10022
Paperback Library
Warner Books, Inc.
75 Rockefeller Plaza
New York, NY 10019
Pathescope Educational Films, Inc.
71 Weyman Ave.
New Rochelle, NY 10802
Pathfinder Press, Inc.
410 West St.
New York, NY 10014
Penguin Books
74 Fifth Ave.
New York, NY 10011
Pennsylvania Council for the Social
Studies
Temple University
Pitter Hall
Philadelphia, PA 19122
Pennsylvania Department of Education
Bureau of Curriculum Services
P. O. Box 911
Harrisburg, PA 17126
Pflaum Publishing
104 Fifth Ave.
New York, NY 10011
Pocket Books
630 Fifth Ave.
New York, NY 10020
The Population Institute
Organization Liaison Division
110 Maryland Ave. N.E.
Washington, DC 20002
Prentice-Hall
Englewood Cliffs, NJ 07632
Project on the Status and Education of
Women
Association of American Colleges
1818 R St. N.W.
Washington, DC 20009
Project Woman
22 E. Grand Ave.
Springfield, IL 45506
Public Affairs Pamphlet Series
381 Park Ave. S.
New York, NY 10016

Quadrangle
10 E. 53 St.
New York, NY 10022
Quartet Books, Ltd.
27 Goodge St.
London W1P1FD
England

Racism and Sexism Resource
Center for Educators
1841 Broadway
New York, NY 10023
Random House
201 E. 50 St.
New York, NY 10022
Resource Center on Sex Roles in Education
1201 16 St. N.W.
Washington, DC 20036
Resource Options
1916 Napa Ave.
Berkeley, CA 94707
Rothchild, Nina
14 Hickory St.
Mahtomedi, MN 55155
Rounder Records
727 Somerville Ave.
Somerville, MA 02143
Russell Sage Foundation
230 Park Ave.
New York, NY 10017

Sage Publications
275 S. Beverly Dr.
Beverly Hills, CA 90212
Scarecrow Press, Inc.
52 Liberty St.
P. O. Box 656
Metuchen, NJ 08440
Schloat Productions, Inc.
150 White Plains Rd.
Tarrytown, NY 10591
Schocken Books
200 Madison Ave.
New York, NY 10016
Scholastic Audio-Visual Center
900 Sylvan Ave.
Englewood Cliffs, NJ 07632
Scholastic Magazines
50 W. 44 St.
New York, NY 10036
Science Research Associates, Inc.
259 E. Erie St.
Chicago, IL 60611
SCOPE
Dowling College
P. O. Box 254
Oakdale, NY 11769
Scott, Foresman and Co.
Research and Information Division
1900 E. Lake Ave.
Glenview, IL 60025
Scott, Jean
1215 Lodi Pl.
Los Angeles, CA 90038

Sheed and Ward, Inc.
  6700 Squibb Rd.
  Mission, KS 66202
Simmons, A. C.
  420 Hawthorn Ave.
  Boulder, CO 80302
Simon and Schuster, Inc.
  1 W. 39 St.
  New York, NY 10018
Smithsonian Institution Press
  1000 Jefferson Dr. S.W.
  Washington, DC 20560
Stanford University Press
  Stanford, CA 94305
Steele, M.
  6502 N. 35 Ave.
  Phoenix, AZ 85017
Sussman, Barbara
  18 Tuxedo Dr.
  Melville, NY 11746

Task Force for the Evaluation of
  Instructional Materials
  P. O. Box 4003
  Stanford, CA 94305
Thomas Y. Crowell Co.
  666 Fifth Ave.
  New York, NY 10019
Times Change Press
  P. O. Box 98
  Louisa, VA 23093
Norma Titcomb
  2027 Malakaa
  Honolulu, HA 98622
Training Institute for Sex Desegregation
  of the Public Schools
  Federation Hall
  Douglass College
  New Brunswick, NJ 08903

Ulrich's Book Store
  549 E. University
  Ann Arbor, MI 48104
Union WAGE
  P. O. Box 462
  Berkeley, CA 94701
Unitarian Universalist Women's Federation
  25 Beacon St.
  Cambridge, MA 02138
United Front Press
  P. O. Box 4009
  San Francisco, CA 94140
United States Government listings:
  Department of Health, Education and Welfare
    National Institute of Education
    Washington, DC 20208

Department of Health, Education
  and Welfare
  Office of Civil Rights
  Washington, DC 20201
Department of Labor
  Washington, DC 20210
Women's Bureau
  Department of Labor
  Washington, DC 20210
Women's Program Staff
  Office of Education
  Department of Health, Education and Welfare
  Washington, DC 20202
University Christian Movement in New England
  11 Garden St.
  Cambridge, MA 02138

Vancouver Status of Women
  2029 W. 4 Ave.
  Vancouver, BC
  Canada
Vintage/Random House
  201 E. 50 St.
  New York, NY 10022
Voyager Recordings
  424 35 Ave.
  Seattle, WA 98122

Franklin Watts
  730 Fifth Ave.
  New York, NY 10019
WEAL, Texas Division
  c/o G. Barnstone
  1711 Harold
  Houston, TX 77006
Wells Associates
  P. O. Box 3392
  Beverly Hills, CA 90212
West Publishing Co.
  50 W. Kellogg Blvd.
  P. O. Box 3526
  St. Paul, MN 55165
Westminster Press
  Witherspoon Bldg.
  Philadelphia, PA 19107
Emma Willard Task Force on Education
  P. O. Box 14229
  University Station
  Minneapolis, MN 55414
William Morrow and Co.
  105 Madison Ave.
  New York, NY 10016
Wollstonecraft, Inc.
  6399 Wilshire Blvd.
  Los Angeles, CA 90048

Women in Literature Collective
Box 441
Cambridge, MA 02138
Women on Words and Images
P. O. Box 2163
Princeton, NJ 08540
Womenfolk Song Project
237 W. Lena Ave.
Freeport, NY 11520
The Women's Action Alliance
370 Lexington Ave.
New York, NY 10017
Women's Education Resources
430 Lowell Hall
610 Langdon St.
Madison, WI 53706
Women's Equity Action League
821 National Press Bldg.
Washington, DC 20045
Women's History Research Center
2325 Oak St.
Berkeley, CA 94708
The Women's Kit and More
Ontario Institute for Studies in Education

252 Bloor St. W.
Toronto, Ont.
Canada
Women's Sports Foundation
1660 S. Amphlett Blvd., #266
San Mateo, CA 94402
Women's Task Force
1401 Walnut St.
Berkeley, CA 94709

Xerox Educational Publications
1250 Fairwood Ave.
P. O. Box 444
Columbus, OH 43216

Youth Liberation Press, Inc.
2007 Washtenaw Ave.
Ann Arbor, MI 48104
YWCA National Board
600 Lexington Ave.
New York, NY 10022

Clearinghouse Publications

FEMALE STUDIES VI
**Closer to the Ground: Women's
Classes, Criticism, Programs—1972**

Nancy Hoffman, Cynthia Secor, and Adrian Tinsley, eds., for the Commission
on the Status of Women of the Modern Language Association. (1972) Essays
on women's studies in the classroom, literary criticism from a feminist
perspective, course materials.

FEMALE STUDIES VII
**Going Strong:
New Courses/New Programs**

Deborah Rosenfelt, ed. (1973) Syllabi for over sixty recent women's studies
courses; descriptions of twelve new programs. Introductory essay assessing
recent developments in women's studies.

FEMALE STUDIES IX
**Teaching About Women
in the Foreign Languages**

Sidonie Cassirer, ed., for the Commission on the Status of Women of the
Modern Language Association. (1975) Listings and outlines of courses with
a focus on women offered by departments of French, Spanish and German
in colleges and universities across the country.

FEMALE STUDIES X
Student Work—Learning to Speak

Deborah Silverton Rosenfelt, ed. (1975) The fruits of some five years of
undergraduate women's studies courses on campuses across the country: a
first play, a "group autobiography," poems, short stories, papers.

FEMINIST RESOURCES FOR
SCHOOLS AND COLLEGES
A Guide to Curricular Materials

Merle Froschl and Jane Williamson, eds. (Revised ed. 1977) A selective guide to curricular materials at every level from the elementary school to the university—for teachers, students, librarians and parents who want to challenge sexism in education and create nonsexist and feminist curriculum.

HIGH SCHOOL FEMINIST STUDIES

Carol Ahlum and Jacqueline Fralley, compilers. Florence Howe, ed. A collection of curricular materials in women's studies for and from the high schools including essays, bibliographies, teaching units.

NONSEXIST CURRICULAR
MATERIALS FOR
ELEMENTARY SCHOOLS

Laurie Olsen Johnson, ed. (1974) A collection of materials for the elementary teacher and student, including quizzes, checklists, bibliographies, workbook, model units.

STRONG WOMEN

Deborah Silverton Rosenfelt, ed. (1976) Annotated bibliography of widely available paperbacks to help the teacher supplement the male-biased curriculum: anthologies, autobiography, novels, short stories, drama, poetry.

WHO'S WHO AND WHERE
IN WOMEN'S STUDIES

Tamar Berkowitz, Jean Mangi, and Jane Williamson, eds. (1974) Complete directory of women's studies programs, courses and teachers, arranged by institution, department and instructor.

WOMEN'S STUDIES FOR TEACHERS AND ADMINISTRATORS
A Packet of Inservice Education Materials

Merle Froschl, Florence Howe, and Sharon Kaylen, eds. (1975) Collection of materials—including an hour-long cassette—necessary for organizing inservice education aimed at eliminating sexism in the school.

WOMEN'S STUDIES NEWSLETTER

Quarterly containing articles on new women's studies programs, innovative courses, teaching techniques, curricular materials, book reviews, conference reports, bibliography, job information.